Undefeated

Changing the Rules *and* Winning *on* My Own Terms

SHAUNIE HENDERSON

Creator of *Basketball Wives*

G

GALLERY BOOKS

New York   Amsterdam/Antwerp   London
Toronto   Sydney/Melbourne   New Delhi

G

Gallery Books
An Imprint of Simon & Schuster, LLC
1230 Avenue of the Americas
New York, NY 10020

First Gallery Books trade paperback edition May 2025

GALLERY BOOKS and colophon are registered trademarks of Simon & Schuster, LLC

Interior design by Jaime Putorti

Manufactured in the United States of America

10 9 8 7 6 5 4 3 2 1

Library of Congress Control Number: 203042580

ISBN 978-1-6680-1222-2
ISBN 978-1-6680-1223-9 (pbk)
ISBN 978-1-6680-1224-6 (ebook)

To my father, the first man I ever loved. You taught me life lessons that have helped mold me into the woman I am today.

To my mother, for always being strong, present, and totally dedicated.

To my kids, for loving me unconditionally and without fail. Thank you for making me the proudest mom in the world.

Last, but not least, to my husband, who encouraged and supported me in writing this book. Thank you for always seeing the best in me when I struggle to see it in myself.

CONTENTS

CONTENTS

INTRODUCTION

In November 2009 I woke up in a small, sparely decorated bedroom in the upper-middle-class, mostly Black Los Angeles neighborhood of Ladera Heights. My two daughters were lying next to and on top of me, and my three sons were sleeping down the hall on couches in the converted office. We were sharing a modest three-bedroom house with my parents and my younger brother, Tyrik. It was quite a change from the thirty-one-thousand-square-foot Orlando mansion we had been living in just a few days before, with its massive basketball court, fitness center, and swimming pool. That house had been our home for the past six months and for practically every summer before that.

After almost a year of planning, I had left my husband of nearly seven years, Shaquille O'Neal, along with the life my children and I had come to know. In that moment, moving back in with my parents was the only choice I had if I wanted any peace for myself and my kids.

I told my divorce attorneys I didn't want to fight with Shaquille. I just wanted him to take care of his kids. I didn't care about anything else. I had also told them I didn't want a cent of Shaquille's money, and I meant it. I wanted to be free to have the life I wanted, on my terms, even while raising five kids under eleven.

For years, my role in life had been clear: I was a wife and mother. I was a daughter and sister. Occasionally, I was a fantastic hostess. I cooked meals and took my kids to school and helped with homework and wiped away tears. Now, I was back home with nothing. I'd turned my back on mansions, luxury cars, private jets, and a lifetime of wealth and privilege.

As my marriage unraveled, I knew I had to find a way to establish financial independence. I never wanted to be dependent on a man for money, an identity, or anything else ever again. Despite what the tabloids have said about me, and what the gossips on social media insisted they "knew," I did not walk away from my divorce a rich woman. In fact, apart from money for child support, I didn't walk away from my divorce with *anything* other than my car. So, while the sudden transition from wealth and comfort to sleeping three to a bed with no permanent address was disorienting, it was the first step to regaining my independence and my life, and that gave me the strength I needed to move forward.

With the help of my parents and family, I got my children settled in school, took a deep breath, and set out to develop and sell an idea I'd been thinking about: a reality TV show based on the real-life wives and girlfriends of players in the National Basketball Association. This was a world I knew well because I had lived in it since 2000. I'd attended the championship celebrations and the glamorous parties (and hosted some of my own). I'd gotten to know the wives as they watched their husbands get traded, get injured—and all too often, get caught fooling around with women they met on the road. I was confident that I could create a show that would tell their authentic behind-the-scenes stories in both a thoughtful and entertaining way. That something would become the runaway hit *Basketball Wives*.

But before we get too far ahead, let's set the record straight. Nobody pulled strings for me with TV networks or production companies to get *Basketball Wives* picked up. I did that on my own, through persistence and sheer force of will, because I had to support myself and my children. And I'll guarantee it was fifty times harder because I'm a Black woman who had no experience as a television producer. Nobody gave me anything.

That's one side of me you don't know. There are others.

While I may be on a reality television show and have some social media presence, I'm extremely private. Despite Black women's voices being more important right now than they have ever been in the history of our country, we still live in a culture where someone like me— an outspoken, unapologetic Black woman who tells it like it is—is seen as threatening. So, after I became a public figure and sort-of celebrity in my own right, I became a target. Because I had been so careful to protect my privacy and limit access to my personal life, people who wondered who I was were free to fill in the blanks with whatever fiction they wanted, and the information was usually not complimentary.

That's the main reason I've wanted to write a book for the last five years. I feel the journey I've gone on is worth sharing. I've been on television since 2010, and I'm at a point in my life now where lots of people think they know who I am, but they really don't—because I've declined to tell them. The piece of me you've seen on *Basketball Wives* is just one frame of my entire movie, and it doesn't really show you the many other sides of me. With this book, I decided to do something deeply uncomfortable for someone as fiercely private as myself: tell my story in full, with (almost) nothing left out.

Why am I sharing my journey and struggles now? I think it's important to leave a legacy that will inspire other women, particularly Black women. As a public figure, I have a platform that can be used to both set the record straight and to help people. I want to inspire women to pursue their creative dreams no matter how often others tell them they can't or that those dreams aren't important. I want to let them know there's more than one way to be a great parent. I want to show them that it's never too late to find life-changing love, and to say, "Never compromise on what you believe to be right."

I sound very confident, but I wasn't always this way. In the pages that follow you'll meet a number of different Shaunies:

- Immature Shaunie, trying to figure it all out;
- Still ain't getting it right Shaunie;
- What the hell are you doing Shaunie;
- Bad decision Shaunie; and
- Getting smarter (finally) Shaunie

I cringe a little when I look back on some of these versions of myself, but the rollercoaster ride has still been a good ride, because the version of Shaunie I am today—fearless, book-writing, telling-my-story

Shaunie—evolved from all those earlier versions. It took each and every one of them to get me to the place I am now. Everything I went through, every betrayal and self-inflicted wound, made me who I am today. I'm damn proud of that version. I have become someone who can take every challenge, every peak and valley, as a lesson. I can really take something from every high and low. I guess that's called wisdom.

I get people coming up to me now saying, "Oh my God, I love this new journey you're on. I love this new life you have." I'll be thinking, *You're just seeing the best part. There were a lot of rough parts you don't know anything about.* Up to now, I've been making this pilgrimage in silence. This book is about changing that.

You might have picked up this book because you thought I was going to share dirt about my marriage to, and divorce from, Shaquille. Yes, I've written about my marriage here, particularly what led to its demise, because in order to understand my journey you need to know what I went through and the choices I made during those years. In doing so, I've shared some details about hurtful and embarrassing things that happened while Shaquille and I were married, but I've also tried to be fair and nonjudgmental, focusing mostly on my part of it and how I felt about it. There are many other stories and details about our marriage that will always remain private. Shaquille is still father to our children and an important figure in my life, and he and I have reached a place of peaceful coexistence. I don't want to ruin that. So, while I'm going to be honest, I'm not going to wallow in the mud.

Before I go any further, it's important that I stress that I'm not blaming Shaquille for what happened to our marriage. He did the best he could with the tools he had. So did I. He was trying to be a world-famous, thirtysomething multimillionaire with thousands of women throwing themselves at him, and people in general begging just to be in his presence, while being a husband and a father at the same time. How could anyone possibly know how to do that?

Meanwhile, I was trying to figure out how to be a good wife under circumstances that were more than a little unusual. We both could have made better decisions. Neither of us took the time to invest in our future by seeking marriage counseling, which, looking back, we probably should have. We both thought we were doing "the right thing" by jumping into family life, and we gave it our best. I'm not sure either of us knew what "being in love" felt like, but we loved the family we had made. We didn't have the wisdom we needed at that time in our lives to nurture each other and grow, both as individuals and together, especially when life was so overwhelming. I like to think we've both gained some of that wisdom since we split and went on to invest in our ourselves and our families in new ways.

You might also be thinking that this will be a gossipy book about *Basketball Wives*. Surely I'm going to dish on behind-the-scenes rumors, rivalries, tantrums, and drama, right? *Wrong*. Yes, there have been ups and downs over the years with my beloved franchise, just as there are in any relationship or endeavor. But at the end of the day, I love all the ladies who have been on the show, along with the crew and the entire team that makes the show possible. They're my friends and family, and in my world family comes first. So, while there will be plenty about *Basketball Wives*, I won't be airing the show's dirty laundry.

While this book does cover some moments and observations about my first marriage and *Basketball Wives* in some capacity, it's more than just that. It's not just one or two things. It's multifaceted, just like I am. Because, like you, I'm also more than one thing. I'm a grieving daughter and a loyal sibling. I'm a mom who worries all the time about her now-grown children while taking great pride in who they're becoming. I'm a dedicated mother, creative and successful producer and entrepreneur, and most importantly, I'm a wife again, having married the man of my dreams, Pastor Keion Henderson, in 2022. I've even become first lady of his church, a plot twist I could never have seen coming.

The point is, I'm all those Shaunies and more, but you don't know that because I haven't let you in. That's on me, and it's time for that to change. I'm ready to step outside my bubble and share what I've experienced, who I was, the decisions I've made, and who I am in the process of becoming. I hope you can see a little of yourself in some of my hardships and heartbreaks, understand me a little better, and maybe learn a thing or two about yourself along the way. Or maybe just laugh, shed a few tears, and enjoy the ride.

God knows I have.

Shaunie Henderson
HOUSTON, TEXAS

Undefeated

CHAPTER 1

A CHRISTIAN MOTHER AND A MUSLIM FATHER

The neighborhood I grew up in from the time I was six set the tone for who I became as an adult. It was working class and mostly Black, but everybody knew each other. Everybody looked out for each other. The phrase "it takes a village to raise a child" definitely applied. The families of our neighborhood broke bread together, kept an eye on all the kids as we ran around playing, and kept their homes and yards clean and tidy. Even though I didn't know it, I think part of the template for my life was set down there: *Be humble. Treat everybody with respect. Take care of your business.*

I'm the oldest of three children. Well, technically five, but that's complicated. My dad had two other daughters by another woman— my half sisters—but they weren't really a part of our lives when I was growing up. I grew up with two other siblings: my sister, Cori, who is six years younger, and Tyrik, who is *eighteen* years younger than me.

For a while I was an only child. That meant I got all the attention, and I loved it.

My dad, Vester Nelson, was a Muslim and member of the Nation of Islam—a very seventies-cool cat, a dedicated pot smoker with a big Afro. My mother, Mary, was, and still is, a devout Christian. While I grew up in a fairly unconventional family situation, all in all, the two competing faiths in our house coexisted pretty smoothly.

My mom took great pains to braid my hair beautifully every day, but I was definitely a daddy's girl. My mom was the one who ferried me to all my activities when I was growing up, but my dad was the one who made me feel special. When I was in preschool, he would pick me up to go and do fun stuff. In keeping with his Muslim faith, he was extremely strict about how a girl should act and who she could be alone with, but he was also warm, attentive, and caring. He was very protective and had strong opinions about the activities I would be allowed to participate in, but he was never stern or a bully. He was just fun to be with.

By the time Cori came along when I was six, my dad was getting active in Islam. I was too young to understand it, but later I would learn that my mom had tried for a year to live a Muslim life, going to mosque and supporting her husband. But she just wasn't happy with it. She didn't believe what they believed; it wasn't how she was brought up. She was trying to follow her husband and be a good wife, but she had been raised a Baptist and wanted to go back to her roots. They talked it over and they agreed that my mother would go back to the faith she'd been raised in. My mom is a classically trained pianist and a singer, and she grew up playing in her church. She went back to her Baptist church, where she played the piano, and my sister and I went with her twice a week.

Being raised in two faiths was never a burden. In fact, it was interesting. On the Baptist side, I went to vacation Bible school and Sunday school and things like that. I enjoyed it because that's where a lot of my friends were. It was more fun than going to Muslim services with my dad, which I also did, because of the strict mandate I was expected to follow. I had to wear the conservative garments that all Muslim women have to wear, which were sometimes hot and uncomfortable. I only went to mosque for the short time my mom went, and I remember that the men and women sat separately.

My dad followed the teachings of the Nation of Islam to the letter. He would buy his bean pies, support *The Final Call*, and be at the mosque every Sunday in his bow tie. He prayed the required five times every day. He would wash up and go in his room and pray on the floor, facing east toward Mecca. That was his ritual. He would also participate in Ramadan every year. He was very disciplined about his religion and read the Quran every day.

He also spoke Arabic on occasion. If you came to our house to visit, he would greet you in Arabic. We could hear him pray in Arabic or speak it to some of his fellow brothers. He wasn't fluent, but it was still impressive to hear him converse in this ancient language. While he didn't require any of us to follow his religion, he did want us to learn about it. We were a sit-down-at-the-dinner-table-and-talk kind of family, and sometimes during dinner or homework, we would have conversations about Islam. We asked him questions, and he would teach us some of the beliefs, some of which I thought were very worthy of respect.

My dad was always immaculately groomed. He shaved every day and polished his shoes. As a little girl, I was obsessed with the process of polishing shoes because he did it old school, with the polish, buffing, shining, the brushes, and the little wooden case that he could put his foot on. He would even shine my penny loafers, because I went to a private school and had to wear a uniform.

I used to get so annoyed because the other kids would get their penny loafers all messed up on purpose. They wanted them to look distressed because that was the cool look. But as soon as mine got a scuff on them, my dad had them on his shoeshine box and got them back in tiptop shape. That's just who he was. For him, cleanliness was definitely next to godliness.

One thing my father never did was talk down to us for thinking for ourselves, even as kids. We made our own decisions, and he was okay with that, even if it meant going to church every Sunday instead of to mosque. He never talked negatively about church, which made me respect him and his religion even more. He was not judgmental or opinionated about what we did or did not believe.

What was extraordinary about all this was that when it came to religion, my parents never made us take sides. I can't imagine that happening today. My dad taught us what he believed, and my mom did the same, but they gave us the freedom to decide what doctrine we wanted to follow, even if that meant following no faith at all. Neither of them ever questioned me about my beliefs. My sister, brother, and I were free to believe in whatever we wanted. My parents always instilled in us that there is a higher power, but how you choose to interact with that power is up to you. Given how divided our country is today, I think it's remarkable that neither my mother nor my father tried to convince us they were right. They respected us.

Today, my sister says that she's more spiritual than anything, but leans toward Muslim beliefs. My little brother leans toward the Muslim side too, because he was super tight with our dad, like two peas in a pod. Mom and Dad never made us choose, which is so fair-minded and rare. I will always love them for that. Me, I'm still a Christian, and while I don't go to church twice a week like I did with my mom when I was growing up, I love being married to a pastor, and I love the Lord.

I was the first grandchild born in our family, so everybody spoiled me, including my paternal grandparents. (Mom's parents had died by the time I was born.) I loved it because everywhere I went I was the apple of everyone's eye. They would fuss over me, tell me I was beautiful, and shower me with attention. My grandmother would call me her "princess," and made sure I felt like it. She was into fashion and bought me a couture jacket for my fifth birthday. I could do no wrong in her eyes, and I could have whatever I wanted. She even got me a credit card when I turned thirteen! It was like I was her little doll, so she did whatever she thought would be amazing for her grandbaby. Somehow, with all the gifts she gave me, I managed to stay humble and not become a spoiled brat!

Up until I was six years old we lived in Hollywood, right near the original Famous Amos cookies store on Sunset Boulevard. My dad would go there, sit down with Wally Amos himself, have coffee, and talk for hours. Wally was a neighborhood institution, a former talent agent who started his cookie business with a loan from Helen Reddy and Marvin Gaye.

By the time my sister was born, we moved to Inglewood, a city in southwest Los Angeles County that was also home to the Forum, where the Los Angeles Lakers would play until 1999. We moved to a few different houses as our family grew, but we stayed in Inglewood until my parents moved to Ladera Heights after I left home.

While my mother and father stayed together until my dad died in 2022, in many ways they were vastly different people. Rather than shower us with hugs and kisses, my mom shows her love in the many acts of service she provides. Growing up, we didn't have to make our beds, cook, wash our clothes, or anything like that, because she did everything for us. Even now, if I were to stay at her house for a few days, she wouldn't let me do anything. When I showed up with the kids after I filed for divorce, she was in heaven—there were beds to make, clothes to wash, you name it. That's her way of showing love.

It's funny now, but that hindered me when I went out on my own, because I never learned to do laundry or anything else domestic. She just wouldn't allow it. I remember having to go into the kitchen and watch her cook because she wouldn't teach me how to do it. I'm a good cook now, but I had to learn on my own by trial and error. I wish Mom had taken more time with me in the kitchen so I could really get in there and feel comfortable cooking, because I love great food and making something special for family and friends.

I never learned to iron either, and I'm still terrible at that. Don't ask me to iron anything unless you want scorch marks on part of it and wrinkles on the rest. I always thought Black women were supposed to be great at ironing, but I guess that skipped a generation.

My mom was deeply invested in us. There was nothing she wouldn't do for her family—no drive too long, no bill too high—for us to have the best, look the best, and go to the best schools. We were her everything. But she did *not* play. As young children, we were pretty well behaved, but one reason for that was that you did not want to get in trouble with her.

Once, when I was in the ninth grade, my friends talked me into ditching class and taking the bus to the mall. When someone from the school called my mother and told her I had missed fifth period, she left work and drove to my school, and when I got back, she was sitting outside waiting for me with a look I'll never forget. My heart dropped to my toes. Set up the firing squad. If my dad had found out, he would've been disappointed and upset and I would've gotten a lecture. But with my mother, ain't no telling what would happen.

I got in her car and we drove off. She was steaming. I could feel the heat coming off her. About ten minutes from school, she started fussing. Then her fussing became yelling and she started socking me hard on the arm while she was driving. My mother doesn't do anything halfway. If she hugs you, you know you've been hugged. If she hits you, you'll have a bruise. She loves hard, and she disciplines hard, and those punches on the arm hurt. And they were enough. I never cut class again.

My dad was the polar opposite of my mother. Where she would lose her temper when we did something wrong, my father didn't yell. His preferred form of discipline was a long lecture. But you knew when he was angry and disappointed, and there would be some type of punishment—you couldn't talk on the phone, you couldn't go out, that sort of thing.

But most of the time my dad was affectionate to a fault. He was always the one saying "I love you" and giving us words of encouragement as we went out the door. If we had something special going on, like a school performance or a final exam, my mom would say, "I'm going to say a special prayer for you" and move on. Not my dad. He would sit us down and we would talk about what was coming up. He took family meetings very seriously, and he believed in sitting down together, communicating, talking things through, and sharing advice. He always made sure to hug us. If we got hurt, he was the one putting the Band-Aid on.

I've taken that lesson to heart with my own kids. I don't get off the phone with any of them without saying "I love you." I don't go to bed without saying it to whoever is in the house. If my big, strong sons are around, I'm kissing them on the forehead, even if it's in front of their friends. They might roll their eyes, but I know they love it. I probably do this because my mom didn't. I always want my kids to know how much I love them, and if I have to embarrass them just a little bit to make sure, I'm all right with that.

Thinking about that reminds me of all the lessons I learned from my parents that I've applied to raising my own kids—including things my mom and dad did that I *didn't* want to do when I became a parent. All of which I'll touch on a bit later.

Since I lived in Hollywood until I was in first grade, and I spent my whole childhood in Los Angeles, I was always seeing famous people. But I don't remember ever thinking I wanted to be an actor or part of the entertainment world. Still, my mom had me audition for commercials and modeling gigs. I did in-store and runway modeling for Saks and Neiman Marcus and even competed on the beauty pageant circuit.

My mom was a *total* pageant mom. We were always traveling to one pageant or another, but this wasn't the creepy pageant stuff you see on some reality shows or documentaries. My mother enjoyed dressing me up, doing my hair, and taking me to competitions, but I don't remember either she or my dad ever taking the whole thing too seriously. It was just fun. I would dance for the talent competition, so my mom always had me in jazz, tap, or ballet class from four years old to when I turned fourteen. I never had a dance routine; I always made it up on the spot and just had a great time. The funny thing was, I would win! We had a house full of little-girl trophies.

Thankfully, I didn't turn into one of those women who's always talking about her long-gone glory days. Nor did I make my own girls compete in pageants in some desperate attempt to relive my past. For my parents, pageants were never about winning, it was about having fun, and all my mom and dad cared about was that I enjoyed myself and had a good experience. Pageant time became playtime! I got to dress up, go out onstage, and smile and wave at people. I was always in shows with the same girls, so we became friends. I didn't even realize it was happening, but while all this was going on I was learning how to conduct myself with class and poise.

Then, when I was in sixth grade, agencies started wanting me to model more mature clothing, like bathing suits. My father put a stop to that. This Muslim man wasn't about to watch his eleven-year-old daughter become sexualized. So much for my budding modeling career!

When I became a teenager my dad laid down strict limits on what I could and could not do. I could hang out with my friends and have sleepovers, go to the movies, things like that. But boys were out of the question. I couldn't go on dates. I couldn't go to dances. I didn't get to go to the prom because that required a date. Of course, like most teenagers, I tried to get around the rules. I would take our phone (the old kind with a cord) from the hallway, sneak it up to my room, plug it into the jack in my wall, and stay up all night talking to a boy I liked at school. I prayed that my parents would stay asleep and not pick up the phone. Once or twice they did pick it up, but I hung up immediately. I think they suspected, but I never got in trouble.

I was never brave enough to ask my dad if I could go on a date because I knew the answer would be no. So, I ended up sneaking around and having "school boyfriends," boys I would just see at school. We didn't go on dates and barely talked on the phone. Those relationships (if you could call them that) usually didn't last very long because most boys didn't have the patience for that type of girlfriend. If I went to the movies at the mall with my friends, a boy I liked might meet me there. I also had godsisters who were older than me that my mom would let me go out with, and they might let me go on a date with a boy on their watch—take us somewhere we could go to the movies or lunch together.

That was my social life when it came to boys. As far as I know, my dad never caught on. I do know that a boy called my house once and my dad scared him so badly he never called again. I don't know what my father said to him, but it was enough that the boy could barely look me in the eye when I got to school. My dad was so serious about protecting my virtue that in tenth grade he enrolled me in an all-girls school. He did not want boys to be a distraction. He was trying to protect me, and now looking back, I'm thankful for his protection and his love.

Through all those years, my parents taught me things they didn't even know they were teaching me. My dad taught me the importance of showing love and affection. Every Friday, rain or shine, he would bring my mother a dozen roses; I always got two roses of my own. Once a week I took ballet, and he would be there watching me dance and taking me out to eat afterward. Sometimes he would pick me up after school on a Friday and take me horseback riding. He always came through when he said he would.

My mother did the same thing. She put a lot of effort into making sure she exposed us to a lot of things as kids, and I'm grateful for that. She took us to dance classes and gymnastics. My sister learned how to play the flute, while I learned how to play the viola. Mom wanted us to get our hands dirty and see what we liked. She took us to plays and made sure we saw *Cats*. That's who she was. She would take off work early to make sure she was able to get her hair done and that we were dressed nicely, and then get us to the Pantages Theatre in time for the opening curtain.

While my father did his best to attend our activities and share experiences with us, it was Mom who did all the driving. It meant so much to me that she worked a nine-to-five job and still made time to drive us to the other side of Los Angeles (which, if you know the city and its awful traffic, is not a small thing) to get us to ballet class, and then sat in the parking lot or in the little waiting area until we were done. I also appreciated that my father always took time to do something special with me. The *effort* mattered. It showed me they loved us. Sure, being dragged to so many different activities was tiring sometimes, but the fact that my parents cared enough to pay for them and commit their time to being part of them was as important as them being in a certain room at a certain time.

When my kids were younger, I was constantly negotiating where I would be and who I would be with, and I made sure they knew about it. I wanted them to see that I was putting in the effort. The conversations would sound a little like merger and acquisition negotiations on Wall Street: "Myles has a play and you have a basketball game, but you also have a basketball game tomorrow. So, I'm going to go to Myles's play tonight because that's only tonight, and I'll be at your game tomorrow, okay?" I'd go to the play and then the game, and everybody would be happy. My kids saw me trying to show up to everything I could. I wasn't trying to score points; I wanted them to see that I really cared.

When I was older, I talked to friends about their experiences growing up and found out theirs had been different from mine. They had parents who worked all day, just like my mother and father, but when the end of the day came, their parents just sat in front of the TV, leaving the kids to fend for themselves. My mom and dad never did that. My mom made sure we did our homework, and my dad made sure we always communicated about things. We were a "together family." Those experiences taught me that I was important, and that spending time together was important. I'm sure that helped me develop strong self-esteem.

Also, when I was a kid, my parents were always helping other people in our tight-knit neighborhood. We might be on our way out the door to go to the movies and the phone would ring. Someone would be calling my father because their power had gone out, they had a flat tire, they needed a ride, or something like that. We would always end up canceling our plans to go help them. I would be sitting in the back seat, thinking, *Come on, I really wanted to see this movie! Do we really have to do this? Can't someone else do it?*

I didn't understand then how special my parents were for being so selfless, but I do now. They instilled that same instinct in me. I will drop everything to help somebody. My father also taught me to communicate and ask questions, never to just accept what I was told. One time he said to me, "Never let someone tell you something that doesn't make sense. Ask questions until it makes sense to you, no matter what that means. Don't ever let somebody tell you two plus two equals five." To this day, I'm a car salesman's worst nightmare.

I don't have to agree with what you're saying, but that's okay as long as I don't walk away confused. I will ask questions until I understand everything that's going on. I taught my kids the same lesson about school. If they complained that they didn't understand an assignment, I would say, "Did you ask any questions?" If they told me they hadn't, I would say, "Tomorrow, you don't leave Ms. So-and-So's class without understanding what she's asking you to do. You're unable to do the work because you walked out of that class without understanding." They would go back and ask questions until they knew exactly what the teacher was asking of them.

If you're thinking I had a storybook childhood, you're sort of right. They might have been a little too strict, but with their words and actions my parents taught me that I was loved and special, that I was talented and smart, and that I had the right to make up my own mind about things, not to be told what to do by someone else. They taught me to respect all faiths, and they kept me safe, even if I sometimes felt restricted socially. However, there were things about my upbringing that I did differently when it came to my own kids.

One of those differences is in how I've prepared my daughters to be on their own. By doing everything for us, even though she meant well, my mom didn't prepare us to solve our own problems. I want my girls to be resourceful and brave. My oldest daughter, Amirah (who I call Mimi), is in college as I write this, and my baby, Me'arah, will be a few months from starting college by the time you read this. I want them to know how to wash clothes, cook meals, and clean up. They grew up in homes where there were always housekeepers and personal chefs, but I'm determined that they learn the skills I had to teach myself. You can't do everything for your children, no matter how much you want to, or you make them helpless.

I confess that when I became a single parent, I may have disabled my own children's resilience a bit by overcompensating. For a long time I felt terribly guilty about breaking up our two-parent home, so I coped by trying to solve every problem for them. If one of my kids had something wrong at school, even though I knew it would be better for them to handle their personal business, I still stepped in and fixed things. I couldn't help it. I'm sure it was a habit I picked up from my mother, and I guess I have no business complaining about it now. But it won't surprise me if when I have grandchildren one day, they call me to make their dentist appointments for them!

However, if there's one important lesson from my upbringing that I've tried to pass on to my daughters, it's how a woman should expect to be treated by a man. For a girl, your relationship with your father is the first relationship with a man you will ever have, and it will shape your relationships with men for your whole life. My father was fun, attentive, and loving to a fault, and he always treated me with affection and respect. That became what I believed I deserved from a man, and that's how I knew Keion was the right man for me. I don't believe I would be with Keion today if my father hadn't shown me that a man could treat me like I was precious—with love, thoughtfulness, and respect.

My parents weren't perfect. For one thing, my dad was *always* late picking me up. Every single time. Like I said, my parents were wonderful about taking us places and doing things with us, but my father just could not be on time. He was usually the one to pick me up at school, and he was often so late getting there that not only would all the other parents and the late school buses be gone, but all the teachers and administrators would be gone too! I would be waiting inside the school with a custodian keeping an eye on me when my dad finally rolled up, two or three hours after everyone else had gone home. It was just something I got used to.

I never felt like he didn't love me because he was so late, because he made me feel so loved the rest of the time. But I never quite understood why it wasn't important for him to be on time. He had to know that time was passing, and that he had to be *somewhere*. The thing you must understand is that my father was an incredibly social and charismatic man, and when he was talking with friends (or even with people he'd just met) time lost all meaning. His routine was to go for coffee at the coffee shop near our home, and at that shop there was a group of older gentlemen who played chess every morning. Naturally, they were all old friends and had a million stories.

Well, God forbid my dad stopped at that coffee shop before coming to pick me up from something! But truth be told, if he stopped at the local newsstand, the story would be the same. He would wind up deep in a conversation that would go on for an hour or more, and then at some point he would glance at his watch and say, "Oh man, I was supposed to pick my daughter up two hours ago! Let me get out of here." And off he would race to get me.

So I knew my father wasn't being neglectful, and he wasn't disrespecting my time. Nine times out of ten he was late because he was chatting with someone or taking a business call and lost track of time. He would pull up, give me an apologetic smile, and say, "Ah sweetie, come on, let's go home. I'm not going to talk about it." I grew up believing that good parents showed up. They made time. My mom worked too, so she and Dad had to trade off handling things like driving me to cousins' houses. Of course, I learned later that not all parents did that.

As teenagers my kids were friends with the two sons of a famous pop singer who I won't name. My sons went over to their house one day, and when they came home they informed me, wide-eyed, that the kids lived in a huge townhouse where the bottom floor was basically the boys' apartment. Mom, the pop star, lived on the fourth floor and she and her sons didn't share anything; in fact, they barely saw each other. My boys, sixteen and seventeen at the time, were a little in awe of this freedom. Not me. I also knew that the pop singer was on tour half the year, and when she was away the kids were left on their own or with a "personal assistant."

"Listen," I said to my boys. "You get that idea out of your head right now because that's never going to happen in our family. I'm going to see your face every day. I need to hear and know what's going on in my house."

But it was in their marriage that my parents had a rough time. As I wrote earlier, my father had two daughters with another woman, one younger than me and one older. That was a wound in their marriage that never healed. My mother was a stand-by-your-man kind of woman—in sickness and in health and all that—but my dad's infidelity left a bitterness in her that never went away, even to the day he died. She believed in family and in making a marriage work, whatever the cost, and that's exactly what she did. It was the same with my dad; he was all about family. There was *nothing* he would not do for his children. He admitted that he might not have been the best husband, but my mom's anger definitely helped him become a better one.

But when I was young, before my sister and brother were born, I witnessed some heavy arguments that I didn't understand, even though I got used to them. Then, when my sister was born, the fights got worse. I still didn't understand them, and that was scary. Eventually, I realized that these terrible arguments were about infidelity—the fact that one or both of my half sisters had been born to a woman my father had an affair with.

Despite this, my parents were determined to stay together, and they did for more than fifty years. However, my mother never stopped being angry at my father. I was just a little girl, not really understanding what was going on, but even I could see the anger in her face. I remember finally saying one day, "Mom, we'll just leave. I go to school with plenty of people whose parents aren't together. You're just so angry at Dad all the time, why don't we leave him?" I just assumed I would be going with her, but of course, she wouldn't leave. It wasn't even an option.

Because of this I grew up in a strange home of loving, involved parents who loved each other, but where my mom *never* let go of her rage. She was never able to forgive my father, and I don't understand why. A lot of people misunderstand forgiveness. They think it's weak—that you're letting the other person "get away with it." That's wrong. Forgiveness puts the person who hurt you in your debt. But it's also a gift to yourself. Forgiving frees you from all those negative emotions. But my mother could never manage that kind of grace. For years she held on to her anger. She loved my dad and was determined to stay with him, but that piece of her that clung to that anger had to make her unhappy. I don't know why she couldn't let it go.

Witnessing this, I decided I would never let my significant other turn me into an angry woman. That's why I eventually forgave Shaquille for the things he did wrong in our marriage. That's a gift I gave to myself.

After graduating from high school I attended community college for two semesters, but school just wasn't my thing and I didn't enjoy it. I went because it was expected of me and I wanted to please my parents, but it also gave me something to do until I figured out what came next. At that time I had no idea what I wanted to do with my life.

After my second semester, I got a job in the marketing department at 20th Century Fox. Being hired was a fluke; I was looking for a job and a friend of mine told me they were hiring. While I didn't really know much about marketing, I applied for the job and got it. When I started, I thought I might still go back to school, but the job and the money were good, so I never went back.

When I took the Fox job, I wasn't thinking "I'm going to be working in Hollywood." In fact, once my modeling and pageant days ended, Hollywood never even crossed my mind. It was fun doing marketing for movies and getting to be on studio backlots, but I still never considered entertainment as a career. I stuck with that job through having my first child, my son Myles, and I was still working at Fox when I met Shaquille and began a whole new phase of my life.

CHAPTER 2

THE EARLY YEARS
AS AN NBA WIFE

Because my father was so strict about boys and dating when I was young, I wasn't remotely prepared for the charm offensive that Shaquille put on when I first met him.

We met in 1999 when I staffed the premiere of *Star Wars: Episode 1–The Phantom Menace* for Fox. I was checking in special guests, and Shaquille wasn't even on the guest list, but he was such a big deal in L.A. that nobody cared when he showed up unannounced. My bosses let him in the theater, but he ended up spending most of the movie in the lobby, trying to talk to me.

Growing up in Los Angeles, I'd always seen celebrities out and about, so the fact that he was famous didn't impress me any more than all the gaudy jewelry he was wearing. I also wasn't into basketball at the time, so while I knew who he was, I was anything but starstruck. But he was just so charming and funny that I couldn't help but enjoy his company. At one point he pulled up a folding chair and sat there, and we just chatted. He kept me laughing the entire time, and eventually he asked me to dinner.

At first I said no. I knew enough about NBA players to know their reputation was that they weren't just players but "players," with a girl in every city, and I wanted no part of that. But we talked for another hour and a half and before he left he said, "Let me take you to lunch." We exchanged numbers and I figured that was that. I was thinking, *He must do this all the time—meet a woman, charm her, and then move on to the next one.* But he contacted me the next day, again asking me to meet him for lunch. I told him I had a full-time job and couldn't just leave my office for a few hours to have lunch, which was hard for him to get his head around. Finally, we found a time to meet, and in between he sent me songs, texting me supersweet and charming stuff. I just kept thinking, *Who is this guy?*

Our first date was lunch at Houston's in Century City Mall. Shaquille was very charismatic and funny and we had a really good time. A few days later, he asked me for another date, leaving me messages where he sang songs to me about liking me. It was hard not to fall for his charm.

On our next date, Shaquille had his chef cook us lunch. I came to his house on my lunch break. After we ate and spent an hour or two together, I announced, "I've got to get back to work." Shaquille was dumbfounded.

"You're going back to work?" he said, incredulously. He seemed almost insulted that I was going back to my job. "You can't just stay and hang out with me the rest of the day?"

I told him I couldn't, that I had bills to pay and a son to take care of, and then I thanked him for the meal and left. I thought maybe he was out of touch with how us mere mortals lived, but that wasn't it at all. Later, I found out that while my leaving was odd to him, he respected it. He told me, "I've never dated anybody who didn't ask me for money. That makes you so different from anybody else." That's a sad and lonely way to live, but it honestly never occurred to me to ask him for anything. While it was never intentional, I think that made him like me even more.

For our next date Shaquille invited me to a Lakers game. He had the usher bring me a dozen roses at my seat during the game. He gave me so much attention during our courtship that he really won me over. When he would buy me a new car he would park it in front of the house with a bow around it. If we went to dinner, the car would be outside when we were ready to leave, with the bow on it so everyone could see how much he loved me. Whenever he gave me gifts (which was all the time) it was always a spectacle. Let's say it was Valentine's Day and he wasn't in town because he was traveling with the team. I would wake up and go downstairs for breakfast and my kitchen would be full of gifts. He loved grand gestures, even if he wasn't there to witness them.

The other thing that made me fall for him was how good he was with my son Myles, who was two at the time. He would say, "Let's go to dinner, and you should bring Myles." Myles was barely walking and still in diapers, but Shaquille wanted him to come, and he loved on him so much that most people to this day still think he's Myles's biological father.

Fast-forward: one year later I was pregnant with our first son, Shareef.

•   •   •

Of course, I had already had a baby, but I learned quickly that it was something different to have a baby with Shaquille O'Neal. I had one of the best ob-gyns in Los Angeles. I toured a hospital VIP area that I didn't even know existed, because you don't get offered that with regular insurance. I had a whole wing of the hospital to myself. It was incredible.

The day I went into labor, I wasn't feeling well. I was going to take a walk, because the baby was due and I was huge, and walking was more comfortable than sitting. My mom came over, as did my girlfriend Alicia, and one of Shaquille's assistants, just in case. At the time, I lived in a high-rise on Wilshire Boulevard, one of the busiest streets in L.A. I walked along Wilshire for a couple of hours and started cramping, so I went to the emergency room. But I was not dilated enough to be admitted, so they sent me home.

A few hours later the contractions started coming hard, and I went back to the hospital. Meanwhile, Shaquille was playing in a game, so he couldn't come. He didn't even know anything was happening. Finally, the game ended, someone let him know I was in labor, and he raced to the hospital. Meanwhile, I was in *pain*, but I was resisting getting an epidural. Eventually a nurse walked in while I was on my side breathing through the contractions, tears streaming silently down my face. She leaned over to me and said, "Sweetie, why are you letting yourself suffer like this? You can have an epidural and not be in this kind of pain."

I told her I was scared to have an epidural, that a needle in my back would hurt so much, that I was afraid I would be paralyzed. Then

Shaquille walked in with my mom, my dad, and Alicia. He was very quiet because he didn't know what to say or how exactly to help. He gave me a kiss on the cheek and sat down next to me, and I agreed to have the epidural.

A few minutes later the nurse walked in with the epidural set up on a tray. I couldn't see it, but Shaquille said "Goddamn" when he saw the size of the needle. My mom snapped, "Shaquille, don't do that." She was holding my hand and when she saw the needle she started squeezing the hell out of my hand. She could see what was about to happen, and her eyes were bugging out of her head. But she kept saying, "It's fine, everything's going to be fine," which just made me more terrified. Then I got the epidural and it was the best thing I ever did.

Now it was time to push. I pushed, and Shaquille, thinking he was being funny, sang "Push It" by Salt-N-Pepa. Excuse me, I am actively working at having this baby right now! But there he was, cracking jokes and cracking up the nurses. After maybe fifteen or twenty minutes of pushing, out came Shareef. Shaquille was *so* proud. He had already had a daughter when I met him, but this was his first son, and Shareef was his pride and joy. He loved being able to say that he had a baby boy.

One thing I learned right away when Shaquille and I started dating was that there is a *definite* hierarchy among the women partners of NBA players. When you're a "girlfriend," traveling with the team, hanging around the hotel, or at the games, the other players' wives don't entirely respect you. Most of the wives either ignored me or were rude and dismissive. It was a nasty, catty competition over who had status and seniority. These women would battle over whose wife sat closest to the team bench, who was allowed to sit in the family section, and that sort of petty nonsense.

John Salley's wife, Tasha, was an exception; she was welcoming and warm to me from the beginning, but that's just her personality. Cookie Johnson, Magic's wife, was also very sweet to me when I was a girlfriend. She knew how the other wives were treating me, so she would pull me to the side sometimes and show me extra love. I was nobody to her, and she didn't have to do it, but she did. Cookie is a class act.

At first I thought all this posturing and dismissing me was just about power games, but then I figured out the real reason they were shunning me. NBA side pieces were (and still are) a dime a dozen. These wives had seen so many young women come and go that they figured any new girl who didn't have a ring on her finger would be gone in the next twenty-four hours. Why bother getting to know her or investing in her if she's just going to be kicked to the curb by the end of the road trip? And so the wives treated me, and others like me, as though we didn't exist and didn't matter. When the Lakers played the Indiana Pacers for the championship in 2000, and I went to Indianapolis with the team, none of the wives even spoke to me.

Not much changed when Shareef was born. In their eyes, I was just a baby mama. Once I had an engagement ring on my finger, things defrosted—but not much. Shaquille's proposal was not the dramatic affair you might expect. I had gone on a trip to the Bahamas with my sister, my cousin, and Alicia. We had a great time, but I was getting really bad headaches. I suffered from migraines a lot back then, so I wasn't too worried, but I thought, *Let me take a pregnancy test because I'm always pregnant anyway.*

Positive.

When I got home, I specifically asked for Shaquille to pick me up from the airport so I could tell him. I got in the car, and I don't know if it was the look on my face or what, but he said, "You're pregnant." I said I was, and he said, "Well, I guess we should just go ahead and get married." That was my proposal, in the passenger seat of a Hummer driving home from Los Angeles International Airport. Be still my heart.

But just being engaged still wasn't enough for the NBA wives. Once we set a wedding date, things got a little better; I was at least semipermanent. But I still wasn't invited to the ball. It was like, "Well, maybe you can come to every other event." I wasn't fully in the club. Then when the wedding invitations went out, the wives started to say, *She must be here to stay, at least for a while.*

It wasn't until we finally said "I do" the day after Christmas in 2002 that I was finally considered a full-fledged member of the NBA wives' club. Our wedding was a little more planned than the proposal. I was very pregnant with Shaqir at the time, so Alicia and our wedding planner took over. I was never one of those women who had her dream wedding all planned out in her head, and I just remember the wedding planner asking me, "What about this?," "What about that?," "What do you think about this venue?" I said "Sure" to everything.

The wedding was elaborate, and I was overwhelmed with trying to get a wedding dress that would accommodate my, um, *changing dimensions.* The person who was making the dress didn't live in Los Angeles, so as I got bigger the dress didn't fit because she couldn't keep up with my growing belly. The wedding planner picked everything, and I just sat back and let it happen because at that moment I knew I was way out of my league.

As you might expect, money was no object, so the budget quickly got out of control. I never saw numbers, but I remember Shaquille's money manager at the time saying to me, "I don't know if you guys know, but you're spending a whole lot of money here." It made me uncomfortable to think people would think I was spending Shaquille's money like water.

Still, our wedding at the Beverly Hills Hotel was beautiful. Everything was over the top. Minister Louis Farrakhan spoke to honor my dad. Yolanda Adams and Luther Vandross sang, and Howard Hewett sang at the reception. Jeanie Buss, who owned the Lakers, was there. Vivica Fox was there. Lakers coach Phil Jackson and most of the players were there. There were paparazzi, helicopters buzzing the hotel—the full Los Angeles celebrity experience.

It was the middle of the NBA season, so we couldn't take a honeymoon. Instead, we spent the night at the hotel and the next day Shaquille had to go back to business as usual. So I went home and everything went back to normal. The following April, Shaqir was born.

Being married finally legitimized me in the eyes of the other NBA wives. A couple of them even apologized for how they had treated me. They said things like, "I didn't think you were going to be around, because the last girlfriend was here for a year and a half, and we befriended her, and then she was gone." I accepted every apology. My philosophy was, *I'll remember how you treated me, but I don't want to live in the past. Let's just move on.* And that's exactly what I did.

In retrospect, it bothers me that I let myself be defined by the man I was with. I wouldn't even think about allowing that today.

From the time we started dating, I knew Shaquille wanted to have a big family, with lots of kids. I have often thought that his own upbringing made him cling to the idea of family. He grew up in a military family, raised by his stepfather, Phillip Harrison, a career sergeant in the army who most people came to know as "Sarge." Sarge was a tough parent, extremely strict, and I think Shaquille hungered for the kind of warm, loving family he hadn't experienced.

His idea of showing love to his kids mainly involved showering them with material things and making sure they never wanted for anything. He has a big heart. At Christmastime especially, he enjoyed doing the shopping and grandly presenting everything, because he *really* loved giving gifts. There are so many fathers who don't fulfill even that obligation, so early on I didn't see that as a problem.

Shaquille showed up as a parent as best he could. He got to be the fun parent; that was how he connected with the kids emotionally. Every now and then he would put his foot down about certain things, but I was primarily the disciplinarian.

In Shaquille's defense, he traveled with the team, so he was on the road a lot. Even when the team was home, he was at practice most of every day. When he'd come home, he would take a nap, have dinner, and then sometimes he would go and work out. He did the best he could based on the demands of his job.

He also enjoyed moments when he felt like he was really taking care of everybody—more than just financially. In 2006, my paternal grandmother passed a few days after I had Me'arah, and Shaquille took care of everything. He flew out with me and the kids, and we were in a hotel for a week while he helped my dad plan the funeral. It's always made him feel good to take care of people.

At this point, early in our marriage, there might have been signs that things weren't quite right, but I didn't notice them. I was just happy. I was living in a mansion and married to a guy who was treating me very well. He did tend to "go missing" a lot, which was strange and which I chose to overlook. At ten at night he might have to go and work out, or go to the gym to put up some shots. He was a professional basketball player, one of the best in the world, so I didn't question it.

Maybe I was naive, but I was hoping for the best. I also made the mistake of thinking that marriage would make Shaquille focus exclusively on me and our family. I developed a blind spot to what were probably signs that things weren't right. I think I was just head-over-heels happy and had so many goals and hopes and dreams for our family that I wasn't paying careful enough attention.

Plus, Shaquille was so attentive and made so many thoughtful gestures. I could be sitting in my seat in the Staples Center, and he would wave to me from the floor or blow me a kiss from the bench. He definitely wasn't hiding me. People knew I was his wife and that we had kids together. What could possibly be wrong?

I was an NBA wife, with all the privileges that came with the title. We lived in a magnificent home in Beverly Hills. I threw parties for other players' families. I went out of my way to learn the names of everyone who worked at the Staples Center and to be nice to them, because I was raised to believe everyone deserves to be treated with respect.

When Gary Payton and Bryon Russell came to the Lakers in 2003, I threw a welcome party for them at our house because I wanted it to be known that I operated on a different level from some of the other wives. I served two different menus—one for the adults and one for the kids—and we had lots of great music and cocktails. I went all-out. I just wanted to be a different kind of NBA wife and to treat other women better than I'd been treated at the start. Later, Gary's wife, Monique, thanked me for making them feel so welcome. She's one of my closest friends to this day; her adult kids still call me "Auntie," and her grandson, Jacoby, is Keion's and my godson.

For me, daily life mostly meant being at home with the kids, who kept me busy all day long. When they were little I didn't take them on the road very often. At that age they didn't enjoy long trips and managing so many little ones on a plane was a lot. Instead, I would pick one or two team road trips—usually to cities where we had family—and the kids and I would fly out and meet Shaquille there. We weren't allowed to fly on the team plane unless it was the playoffs or the finals.

If the kids weren't traveling with me, I might leave for just three or four days (league road trips were often ten or eleven days long), meet Shaquille in a city I knew I would enjoy, and we would have some quality time together.

Looking back, I don't know that I was ever really in love with the man, but I was in love with the idea of being married to the man I had a family with. I was in love with the idea of building a life together. I truly did enjoy spending time with him. Road trips gave me a chance to be with my husband and experience the NBA life for a little while.

I also went on road trips to get Shaquille's full attention. At home there were so many distractions, but on the road it was just the two of us. I really did enjoy that. I also got a break from the kids, which was always nice. My mom would look after them so I could catch my breath. I also got to spend time with some of the other wives. We'd sit together at games, and while the guys were at practice we would go shopping or have lunch. We understood each other's schedules and lives, so it worked out perfectly.

If I did bring the kids with me, we might travel to New York, because New York was always fun. Shaquille's family lived in New Jersey back then, so if his team was playing the New Jersey Nets, the kids would come with me so they could visit their grandparents. We also had a house in Orlando, so if the team was playing the Magic, we would fly out and stay at the house and I would take the kids to Disney World, which of course they loved.

I took the kids on the road because they thought it was an adventure, not because they were crying for their dad. I'm sure they missed him, but he was normally away from home so much training with the team or traveling to road games that they were used to him not being there. But when I did take them with me, Shaquille was extremely proud to have them there. He loved to show off his children. He wanted people to see what a good dad he was.

Every now and then, we would travel together as a family. For instance, when Shaquille was playing for the Miami Heat and the team played in L.A., we would always go out to Los Angeles and stay for a week so we could see grandparents and other family. That was always fun. If the trip fell in December, we might have Christmas on the road. A few times we packed up all our Christmas stuff and shipped it to

Los Angeles—and I mean *all of it*. One year we had Christmas in the Beverly Hills Hotel, which was super fun, because the Beverly Hills Hotel at Christmas is next-level festive. You go into the hallway, it's Christmas. Go into the lobby, it's Christmas. Go out to the valet station, it's Christmas. The kids were in heaven. When we lived in Miami, the Beverly Hills Hotel was like our second home.

Thanks to all the travel, the kids became quite familiar with certain cities and learned how to behave on a plane (an important skill even some adults haven't figured out), and they enjoyed traveling as much as they could. But they were still young, and being dragged around to different cities wasn't easy for them.

Honestly, it wasn't easy for Shaquille either. He was on the road most of the time, so he had a lot of time to himself. For him to spend a week in a hotel room with kids running around nonstop was . . . challenging. At home, if the kids were bouncing off the walls, he could get away—go to the gym or another part of the house and have some peace. Not on the road. He loved the kids but having them underfoot for five days was a lot. So, I established a tradition: we would always go on at least two family vacations in the summer, when the NBA was between seasons.

Those were the trips where everyone got what they needed: fun time, sun time, quiet time, and activities for the kids. We went to the Caribbean a lot—Turks and Caicos, the Bahamas, the Cayman Islands—anywhere the kids could spend the entire day on the beach and have a good time. We had some great adventures and did things together that my kids will always remember, like riding a glass-bottomed boat that lets you see all the coral reefs and sea life. We had some awesome times.

And when I say *family vacation*, I mean the whole family. Not just all five kids—Myles, Shareef, Mimi, Shaqir, and Me'arah—but my mom and dad, my sister, and my brother, too. I miss those days because we did a lot as a family. Family is everything to me. There's nothing that feels as good as being around family—playing games, cooking, cracking jokes, just being together. In those years my family was always around. They didn't miss anything. If there was a game or a school play, they would show up. If it was Thanksgiving or Christmas, even if we were living in another city, my parents flew in from Los Angeles.

Those were the good days, the innocent days when summers felt endless. I look back on those days with so much nostalgia. Those were the days before my father passed away, before I got divorced. Before all the kids grew up and moved all over the place. It's harder to be close when everyone has their own busy lives. But God, I loved having family around so often and for so long. I'm glad my kids will always have those memories.

During those years, I worked hard to keep the kids grounded. I had grown up in a comfortable home, but we were firmly middle class, nothing fancy. Other than Myles, my children had never known anything but huge houses with pools and home gyms, private chefs on call, giant televisions, luxury cars, extravagant Christmases, and everything else that NBA money could buy. I did not want all that to go to their heads or make them entitled. I wanted to keep them grounded, humble, and aware of how incredibly lucky they were.

It wasn't easy and I had my work cut out for me. We lived in a mansion, their dad had a dozen cars, I had my fancy SUV, and so on. But day to day, I made choices to be just like everyone else. I wasn't going to walk my babies in a stroller up and down Rodeo Drive, going in and out of Gucci, Prada, and Chanel, which was a thing I had seen some mothers do when they wanted to be seen—when they wanted to be extra and say, "Do you see how wealthy I am?" *No thank you.* I would take the kids out to the Sherman Oaks Galleria, where they could go on a Ferris wheel or a train ride. I definitely did my share of shopping on Rodeo Drive, but I never used those shopping trips as opportunities to be "seen."

It also wasn't always easy to instill good values in the kids, especially since Shaquille spent most of the year wrapped in the NBA lifestyle—private planes, huge hotel suites, people to bring him whatever he needed, and so on. He was no longer connected to how "regular" people lived. He would tell me to go to Bloomingdale's or Neiman Marcus to buy onesies for the kids, and I would say, "Why would I spend a hundred dollars for a silk onesie that the baby's going to outgrow in thirty days when I could get three Carter's onesies at Target for twenty?" Well, he wasn't having any of that. He thought of Target as the place where the poor people shopped, another version of Walmart.

That's why it was so funny one Halloween when he volunteered to go to Target for me. I had forgotten a piece of one of the boys' costumes, but I was also very pregnant with Shaqir, and he didn't want me going out after dark, even though it was only seven or eight o'clock. "No, no, no, no. I'm gonna take care of it," he said. But I knew he had never set foot in a Target before, and I didn't think he even knew how to get to our nearby location. But he was trying to be considerate, so I gave him directions and told him what we needed, and off he went with Myles as his navigator.

Myles was seven or eight at the time, and after he managed to tell his father how to get to Target, he had to lead him around, because while Myles had been to Target with me a hundred times and knew where everything was, Shaquille was completely out of his element.

Picture it. This second grader was leading this giant man around Target by the hand, and all the while Shaquille was looking around wide-eyed, not believing what he was seeing. He called me and he sounded like a kid who had just seen Disneyland for the first time. "Oh my God, they have everything here!" he shouted through the phone. I could hear Myles in the background, getting more and more annoyed as he tried to drag his father over to the aisle where they had the Halloween costumes. "Babe, why didn't you tell me this place had everything? They have drawers (his word for underwear). Did you know that? I could've been coming here the whole time!" He was fascinated by everything, even things he didn't need at all.

I ended up spending twenty minutes on the phone with Shaquille during what should have been a five-minute Target run (I know, I know—none of us ever make five-minute Target runs). He had discovered something new and amazing. When he and Myles came back . . . oh my God. He had bought *everything*. Air fresheners for his car, candles, towels. He bought practically everything they sold at Target on a night when we just needed two things. Target stopped being the cheap place where the poor people shopped and became his *favorite* store.

I think it was that balance of lifestyles that helped keep the kids' feet on the ground. When we visited my parents, the kids saw that they lived a nice, upper-middle-class lifestyle. They weren't living in a mansion. They were living in a nice home in an upscale, mostly Black Los Angeles neighborhood surrounded by regular neighbors, not mansions with walls and automatic gates. When we hung out at my parents' house—which we did probably four times a week—my kids played outside with their neighbors' kids, just like other kids. They were regularly made aware of how drastically different their home life was from how the vast majority of other people lived.

To this day, my kids are still friends with some of the kids they played with back in those days. The kids have all grown up and moved on, of course, but most of their parents and grandparents still live on the same street as my mom. My kids played sports at their schools, which were predominantly white and very upscale. But they also played AAU (Amateur Athletic Union) ball in Baldwin Village, a rough L.A. neighborhood known as the Jungle, which became famous in the movies *White Men Can't Jump* and *Training Day*. They played with teams that were barely able to get the money together to transport these boys to their next game, traveling on whatever airline they could purchase tickets from at the last minute, and staying wherever they could afford to.

I made sure the kids experienced and witnessed life across the socioeconomic board. During the holidays I would say, "Time to clean out the closet. We're gonna take out all the stuff you don't wear and all the things you're done with and take them downtown to the Union Mission and give them away for the holidays." They knew the ritual, and they took a lot of pride in it after they understood what I was doing and why it was important. We would pack everything up and I would take the children to downtown L.A., where we would donate our things and then go to the women's shelter to volunteer to make plates of food for mothers and their children.

Some years we'd go there for Mother's Day, and the kids would see me working in these places, serving others. It got pretty real, because they would see people who were mentally ill and some people who were just angry and didn't care what you did for them. The kids had to get used to what was going on there. They would ask me things like, "Why is this man still mad, even though I gave him a plate of food? Why is he still fussing?" Or, "Why can't I get these little girls to talk to me or look at me? Why are they scared of me?"

It took a lot of conversations. I made sure they saw everything, because I wanted them to understand that they were (and still are) blessed and should always be appreciative of what they have, because most people don't have as much as they do. I needed them to experience it, not just talk about it or see it on TV. I think that that has made them humble, appreciative, and grounded as they start their own adult lives.

Today, as adults, my kids can walk into any room and feel comfortable. They've seen me serving others, and I want them to learn the life lesson of service as well, because we're all here to serve others in some capacity, whether that's physically giving clothes or food to those in need or sharing some wisdom that could help someone in life. I want each of my kids to have an attitude of service, because it's uplifting and fills you with a level of gratitude and appreciation for life that I think everybody needs.

Life at home worked the same way. The unspoken rule was: *Yes, you have a lot of stuff, but that doesn't mean you're better than anybody else.* I was the parent who said no. I would also reference other kids they went to school with—kids whose families were often wealthier than ours. "I know you just saw little Johnny kick his mom in the shin and tell her he hated her. Don't you ever even think about it," and "I know you saw Christina tell her dad she wanted a Ferrari for her thirteenth birthday and get it, but don't even think about it. That's not how this goes over here."

If *Maury* was on TV, I'd call the kids over. "See all those kids who go onstage and talk about where their moms and dads went wrong?" I'd say. "The kid from school who kicked his mom is going to be on *Maury* one day, and his mama's going to be crying, 'Maury, help me. He's out of control!' You will be missing a front tooth before I ever allow you to get that out of control."

Kids need to have a little bit of fear of the repercussions of bad behavior. That's why our household was very balanced. Yes, we lived in a mansion. Yes, Dad is over the top and has more cars than one person should ever have. But we will be respectful and care for each other and for those in need, and never take what we have for granted.

I enjoyed those sweet early years being a mother and raising my children; my days were always busy with kids and family, and every now and then I got to travel or enjoy a little of the NBA high life. But invisibly, my marriage was beginning to crumble.

As I've written, it wasn't obvious early on. You know how when you first get sick, and the symptoms are so mild that you're not even sure you *are* sick? That's how things were in the early years. I was busy and happy and didn't notice what was going on. But as the disease progressed, the symptoms became harder and harder to ignore. Take

Shaquille's habit of "going missing." Our chef did all the grocery shopping. His managers paid all the bills. I took care of the kids. So where was he going in the morning, during the day, and at night? No one works out *that* often. When we moved to Miami, I even heard a rumor that he had a condo in Miami Beach. I started to get suspicious, but he always had an answer, and I could never prove anything.

Eventually, I was forced to admit that my family life wasn't as blissful or perfect as I wanted to believe.

CHAPTER 3

RACISM DOESN'T CARE
IF YOU'RE FAMOUS

When Shaquille was playing with the Los Angeles Lakers, which he did from 1996 to 2004, we lived in one of the nicest parts of the city and sent the kids to the best schools we could find, which were mostly white schools in affluent parts of the area. I won't apologize for this; we wanted them to have the best education possible, like any parents would, and they had a lot of opportunities and wonderful experiences made possible by attending those schools. But because the students and families were primarily white, my kids and I also came face-to-face with racism.

Maybe I was lucky, but I don't recall experiencing racial prejudice when I was growing up, with one exception. I also went to mostly white schools, and tried to please the children who had never had a Black classmate and were looking at me like I was a life-size doll. If they wanted to play with my hair, which was different from their hair, I would let them.

Like many girls, when I was in the seventh and eighth grades, I started to develop curves, but my curves were different from those of a lot of the white girls. The little boys would draw pictures of me on their desks: a stick with a bubble for my butt. That was my first exposure to body shame, and I never forgot it. I was ashamed of my body for so long that into adulthood I wore things to cover my butt and hips, because all the little white boys in middle school made fun of my curves. Even into my thirties, I always wore a shirt tied around my waist to camouflage my butt. I didn't even think about it; I just did it.

Later, I finally developed the literal "kiss my ass" attitude that I have today. Actually, I prefer to call it a "soft 'Go to hell.'" However you label it, I love how I look today, and I'm not concerned with what anyone else thinks. I developed that thick skin by being on TV. Being on-screen gives everyone permission to have an opinion about you. That used to get to me, but then I would ask myself, *Why are you letting their opinions affect you?* These were bloggers or social media influencers whose job was to get people to read their articles or look at their pages, so they were going to say what they needed to say to drive traffic. I stopped taking them so seriously.

When there was all kinds of stuff in the news about him—some of it true, most of it not—Shaquille would say, "Just let it ride. It'll be over, and something else will happen within twenty-four hours that'll knock my story off the block." It's true. You have to master the art of being silent and letting go. If you participate in a critical story, you make it bigger. If you don't feed it, it dies and most people forget it ever existed.

If I need to tell someone politely to go to hell, that's what I'll do. I won't disrespect you or come at you crazy. But I do believe in being honest. If an environment or a situation makes me feel bad about how I look or anything else, I'll walk out. I'm not apologizing for it. And in the end, it saves us all a bunch of time and energy.

I wanted my kids to be equipped with that attitude from day one, to be proud not only of their hair, skin, and bodies but of being Black. I taught them to clap back when kids tried to touch their hair and to go ahead and talk trash on the basketball court, and if some little white boy couldn't handle it, that was his problem.

I have a blessed life, no question. But because of the systemic racism coded into American culture, it would've been a lot easier if I wasn't a Black woman. For every step you take away from the privileged class of our society—straight, white men—access and opportunity become twice as difficult. If you're a woman, you have to work twice as hard as a man to succeed. As a Black woman, I've had to work four times as hard—and as smart—to build what I've built. I resent it, not just for myself, but for the millions of brilliant, hardworking Black women who didn't have the same advantages I had—a strong family upbringing and marketable experience as an NBA wife.

We all deserve better than to have to climb a wall, not just of sexism but of prejudice, to chase our ambitions. I won't apologize for wanting that for myself, my kids, or anyone.

Shockingly, I can only remember one experience of in-your-face racism from my adult life. It was also the only time I have ever been called the N-word to my face. I guess I've just been lucky.

It happened not long after my current husband, Keion, and I got married. We were having a great dinner at one of our favorite Houston restaurants with three other gentlemen and one young lady (we were the only couple, and the only Black folks). This white woman at the bar, who knew some of the people we were having dinner with, came over to say hello. She greeted her friends and went back to the bar. After dinner, the people we were with invited us to join them at a popular piano bar, a local hot spot where lots of people get up and sing. It sounded fun so we said, "Sure, why not?" and went.

While at the piano bar, we were sitting around a small table, having drinks and listening to the music, when the lady from the other restaurant appeared and asked if she could join us. This was pure coincidence. This piano bar was where people in this part of town commonly went after dining out, including this woman. We invited her to sit down, and we three women began our own conversation while the four men talked. But I got a strange vibe from this woman. Her tone was a little snotty toward me and she kept making nasty comments about immigrants. After a while, she and the younger woman (who was very sweet) began having their own private conversation and ignoring me.

After a few minutes, things between them got intense. The white lady from the bar started accusing this young girl of having feelings for the man who was hosting our dinner party. Before I knew it, they were arguing over this man, and things were getting loud. Suddenly the white lady stood up, swaying a little and holding a plate full of shrimp cocktail. Now I could smell the alcohol on her. My reality TV radar was at full power; I had seen this sort of thing before. I leaned into Keion (who had no idea what was happening) and whispered, "Babe, some *Basketball Wives* shit is about to go down."

One of the things I love about my husband is that he always thinks the best of people. He said, "No, babe, it's fine." I'm sure he was thinking what you're thinking: *These are white people. They don't do this kind of stuff in these kinds of places.* Well, in this instance Keion was wrong, because they most certainly do.

Thirty seconds later, the drunk white lady threw her plate at the young woman. Fortunately, the booze had messed with her aim, because the food flew between Keion and me and hit the wall. "I knew it!" I shouted. And with that, everybody stood up, and our dinner host said, "Misty, stop! What's wrong with you? Stop this!" Misty picked up a fork and tried to stab his hand where it sat on the table, but no one did anything. They just stared while Misty swung silverware around, completely out of control.

Keion tried to calm things down. Misty was obviously a danger to everyone, so he quietly circled round behind her and got her in a bear hug. Evenly, he said, "Ma'am, I'm going to let you go, but you can't do this. Let's go outside and talk about it." Misty was having none of it, because she started cussing him out: "Get off me, you blankety-blank-blank!" Now, the bouncer came over and said, "I'll get her." But Keion couldn't let Misty go, because she was kicking, screaming, and making a huge scene.

Finally, the bouncer said, "Can you take her outside?" Keion nodded and started to walk Misty toward the door. She went limp on him, hoping he would drop her, so he was forced to drag her along the floor! Eventually, we all made it outside into the parking lot—me, all these other men and women, and my husband holding the crazy drunk lady. Just then I noticed that Keion's shoe was wet—the woman had urinated on him! This grown woman was standing in a puddle of her own pee, kicking and screaming like a toddler.

I'd had enough. I leaned over to Misty and said, "This is crazy. You've got to stop. If you do, he can let you go." Instead, she started cussing me out. Keion saw, like I did, that she wasn't going to cooperate, so he let her go. Immediately she turned around and started kicking him with her spiked-heel boots. All he could do was try to dodge, because I knew there was no way he would ever hit a woman. But I could. If she was kicking my husband, I'd lay her out. I walked up to Misty and said, "Here's the thing. You're going to stop, or I'm going to have to hurt you, and I don't want to do that."

She said, "You're not going to do shit," and took a swing at me. But she was so wobbly-drunk that all I had to do was put my hand out and she sort of . . . tipped over. Now she was on the ground and completely freaking out. "You bitch! Oh my God, you knocked me down!" I just said, "You know what? I have witnesses who will say I didn't do anything." There were about thirty people in the parking lot by now, and they quickly backed me up.

If there's one thing I can't stand, it's drama. I was *done*. Keion finally said, "Babe, let's just go back inside. They'll take care of this." We started walking away and Misty screamed, "You nigger bitch, bring your nigger ass back here!"

Gasps from everyone who had been watching. Then, silence. *It was on.* I started to take my sweater off. "Now I can whoop your ass and it's justified," I shot back. Fortunately, Keion kept a cool head. He put his hands on my shoulders and gently said, "Baby, do not. Don't entertain it." Surrounding us were all these well-dressed white ladies, and I could tell they were mortified by the whole thing. They were saying things like, "Oh, I'm so sorry . . . She's drunk . . . It's okay, just go inside . . . Don't worry."

I was more shocked than angry. No one had ever spoken to me in such a blatantly racist way like that before, ever. I wanted to knock

Misty's teeth out, but Keion was right. We walked away and went back inside the bar. But when I got back to the table, I didn't know what to do. Was I supposed to turn the other cheek because she was drunk? The old Shaunie would have fought her and felt better.

Later, Keion and I got in the car and were just sitting there, looking at each other and thinking, *What the hell just happened?* The next day, when I told my kids about the incident, they were mad, and they had a plan. They said, "Let's go back there tomorrow. You think she's going to be there tomorrow? Let's all go."

I had to laugh. My kids, ready to defend their mom from drunk racist white ladies. I said, "And what exactly are we supposed to do when we get there?" They told me they wanted to just be there and scare her so she wouldn't ever want to come back there. We didn't go back, but I'm still speechless when I think about what that woman said to me. That's the thing about racism. You're never ready for it. And it's always right there waiting to jump out in front of you.

Before I go on, I want to address something that I'm fairly sure some readers are thinking right now. Here I am, a successful TV producer, entrepreneur, and now author. I'm married to an incredible man. I have five happy, healthy children whose wealthy celebrity father took care of their financial needs. With the amazing life I have, how can I justify uttering a word of complaint about racism, or anything else for that matter?

It's a fair question, and I'll answer it fairly.

Now, whether you agree with it or not, the bottom line is that I don't particularly worry about racism's effect on me. I've been through a lot, and as a result, I've developed a thick skin. I don't like it, but I have more important things to do than sit around and feel like a victim due to someone else's ignorance. I'm too busy keeping *Basketball Wives* on the air, creating jobs by creating new TV shows and launching businesses, being a first lady at my husband's church, and trying to be a good wife. But my children are a different matter.

As almost any parent knows, watching your child suffer is much worse than suffering yourself. Imagine seeing your beautiful Black child called the N-word, your daughter teased because of her elegantly braided hair, or your son pulled over by the police because he was "driving while Black." Imagine the confusion, anger, humiliation, and pain your children feel at being the target of hate and cruelty because of nothing more than their skin, hair, clothes, or what they brought to school for lunch. Multiply that by a thousand and you'll understand why I'm speaking up.

Starting from the time they were small, my kids had to deal with the thoughtlessness of white classmates when it came to hair, clothes, and more. As I noted earlier, there weren't a lot of Black kids at Wildwood School or the other schools they attended, and that led to some misunderstandings. Once, Myles got sent home from school because he was playing basketball on the playground at recess and was talking trash—a totally normal cultural thing among Black kids. You ball, you throw down verbally. You block a kid's shot, you shout, "Get that shit outta here!" It's meant to be innocent fun with a little bit of attitude. But rather than take it that way, one of the white kids told the teacher that Myles was bullying him, and as a result, Myles got sent home.

I explained to my children that when it came to the kids in their schools, "They don't understand you because they think you're different from them. They don't understand your hair. They don't understand how you talk. They don't understand what's in your lunchbox. They don't understand how we function as a family." Repeatedly, I talked to them about issues that I knew other kids, and their parents, wouldn't understand. It wasn't just to avoid conflict, either. They were part of a tiny minority in their schools, and I didn't want them to feel shame over the ways they were different from the other kids. I wanted them to walk the halls of their schools with pride.

I knew what to say because as I wrote earlier, my parents also sent me to predominantly white schools. One thing I remember from those days was that my parents didn't serve us milk with meals. For us, milk was something you put on your cereal. We drank water or juice with our meals. But all the white kids normally drank milk at lunchtime, and schoolchildren are great at detecting anything or anyone that stands out from what's normal, so they made fun of me for not drinking milk. I remember going to my mom and saying, "Mom, I get made fun of because I don't drink milk." She would reply, "Oh, don't worry about them. Don't let them tell you what you're going to do." That was the end of the discussion.

But while kids don't always know they're being offensive and/ or racist, adults do. That's why racism directed by grown-ups at my children is so upsetting to me. Back when Amirah was in second grade, her teacher pulled me aside one morning and said, "Is there anything you could do with your daughter's hair?"

I was taken aback. "What's wrong with her hair?"

The teacher, an older white woman, huffed as she tried to explain. "Those things, the things in her hair, they're distracting." I was confused, because "things in her hair" didn't make sense. I asked the teacher what she meant, and she said, "I could be reading to the class, and then I look up and I see Mimi and these things in her hair, and it just looks like Medusa. They're so distracting to me and my students. Is there something else you could do with her hair?" She was talking about my little girl's braids like they were the snakes coming out of the head of a monster from Greek mythology!

I'm rarely left speechless, but at that moment I had no idea what to say. This was an older lady and a teacher, someone who should have commanded respect, but I couldn't imagine how to tell her that what she had said to me was deeply repulsive without disrespecting her. I was never more offended in my life. I wanted to grab Mimi by the wrist and storm out of the classroom. But eventually I got my temper under control, went out to my car, and called my mom. I told her what had happened, and this Warrior Grandma was ready to come to the school and give this woman a tongue lashing on my behalf!

If you're white, you might not fully understand why what the teacher said was so offensive, but if you're Black, you get it. Black hair is a *big* deal, especially for women. Because Black hair has a unique structure, many women wear it in styles like locs, braids, or twists to protect it from damage. For many women, Black hair (and how we wear it) is also wrapped up in issues of identity, ethnicity, culture, and power. Google "Black women's hair" and you will find thousands upon thousands of editorials and YouTube videos of Black women describing how their natural or ethnically based hairstyles have led to discrimination in workplaces and schools. The Legal Defense Fund of the NAACP is even championing a law called the CROWN (Creating a Respectful and Open World for Natural Hair) Act, which bans race-based hair discrimination.

When someone treats Black hair like a plaything or complains that its appearance is offensive or even frightening, it sets off alarm bells. This comment from the teacher was like an attack on my daughter's identity. After I spoke to my mom and calmed down a bit, I went to the one Black teacher at the school, whom I had befriended, and explained what had happened. Before I could finish my story, she was in tears.

"Unfortunately, I'm not surprised that that comment came from her," she said. "Please take this all the way to the very tip top of whoever will listen." So that's what I did. Long story short, the school ended up sending the teacher to a multicultural conference, which was supposed to help educate her about systemic racism and put an end to her inappropriate cultural comments. But that was just a Band-Aid, like such things always are. You can't change a lifetime of ignorance and bigotry with a mandated class any more than a court-ordered anger management course can make a violent person nonviolent.

I, along with most other Black moms who send our kids to schools with large non-Black populations, am often forced to have frank conversations with them. We say, "They're going to play with your hair. They're going to ask you 'What are these braids?' They won't understand your lips. They won't understand your butt. They won't understand your nose. They won't understand all these things. Just know that you don't have to defend anything or explain anything to them."

I wanted my children to be strong so that their response would be strong. I wanted them to draw a clear line by saying things like, "None of your business," "Don't touch my hair," or "Please don't do that." I didn't want them to be rude or fight, because again, little kids aren't racists. They truly don't know any better. But I wanted my kids to be able to confront children's ignorance in a way that came from a nonviolent place of respect for themselves and their culture.

It wasn't just hair or skin color, either. In school, differences always get made fun of. Your kid's clothes aren't as nice as the other kids' clothes? She'll be teased. Your kid has a speech impediment? He's guaranteed to come home crying more than once. Now, try being some of the only Black kids in a mostly white, big-city public school, with a world-famous father.

My kids were always taller than everyone else's kids. That makes sense, right? Look who their dad is. All four of them inherited the O'Neal DNA. Even Myles, who isn't Shaquille's biological son, is six foot three, and Shareef is six ten. Starting in elementary school, they were always the tallest kids in their class. But while height is cool for a boy, growing up, Mimi and Me'arah hated it.

At one point, Mimi didn't want to go to school because the boys would make fun of the fact that she was taller than they were. Today, she's about six two, but even in the seventh grade, she was about five eight and towered over most of the boys her age. They made fun of her. When you're a kid, you want more than anything to fit in with your peers—not stand out. Mimi was being mocked for something she had no control over.

Being persecuted for your height might not meet the definition of racism, but when you're a child, it doesn't matter. What matters is that my kids were seen as different. Singling them out for their height was another way of playing into stereotypes: all Black people are tall, all Black people are gifted athletes, and so on. When you live in this country, where racism always simmers just below the surface, your radar gets hypersensitive.

During this period I was constantly reassuring Mimi that the other kids were just making fun of her because they were jealous that she was so tall and beautiful. I wanted her to recognize that the things that made her insecure were some of the most beautiful things about her. I always tried to celebrate my kids' differences. I reminded Mimi that she could take the boys in her school in any sport they played. I explained that the boys were just intimidated. "Sometimes, boys think girls are automatically weaker than they are," I'd say, "but look at the other girls. They can't do what you can do."

Still, fifth grade was tough for her. She struggled a lot with her self-confidence. She would say to me, "Why would I want to go in here? They're just going to tease me again." But by the time she got into sixth grade, she had started to develop a little swagger that I was glad to see. I could see her telling herself, *Not only am I taller than the other kids, but I can hit a baseball farther than they can, and I can throw a football farther than they can.* She finally started to find her self-confidence and was able to start seeing the teasing as jealousy.

I had to go through the same process with Me'arah, but she was so athletically talented from a young age that she always had that swagger. But she's a bit of an introvert. She's not one of those kids who will walk into a room and start talking to everybody. She's fine just being quiet. But her athleticism has made her super confident. She doesn't need anybody. She's also probably my most mature kid, because she's seen the mistakes her older siblings have made and learned from them. She'll even call them out: "That was dumb. Why would you do that?" She's the most mature eighteen-year-old I've ever been around.

Over the course of nearly twenty years of sending my Black children to mostly white schools, I spoke over and over again with teachers, administrators, and parents about the same race-related issues I mentioned above. Nothing changed. With each child, I had to have the same conversations with people who just didn't get it. If you're bringing up Black kids, I'll bet you're having those same conversations today. And that's just sad and unacceptable. But at the same time, racism doesn't just come into play at school or in sports.

A Black parent might also have to sit their driving-age sons and daughters down and walk them through how to behave if they get stopped by white police officers for speeding or running a stop sign ("driving while Black")—or for wearing a hoodie in the wrong neighborhood—so they don't get shot. Can you imagine? You can if you're a Black parent. I've had those conversations with all my children, and afterward I couldn't decide if I wanted to cry, scream, or punch something. It's awful, but it's part of the reality we deal with.

As difficult as it is to talk about racism with our children, we must be proactive about it, because we're the ones who deal with the tears, the calls from teachers, and the comments from thoughtless (or straight-up racist) parents. But I knew that while I couldn't change the teachers or parents, I could help my children become better at dealing with and calling out racism. The key word for me was *pride*. I wanted my kids to face ignorance and stereotypes by being proud of who they were— proud of being Black, of being strong, smart, athletic, talented, generous, and hardworking. It was important for me to make sure they knew this wasn't about them. They hadn't done anything wrong. There wasn't anything wrong with them. This was about other people's fear or ignorance, and they could rise above it.

I'm happy to say that strategy has worked. Today, all my children are deeply proud of who they are, and of being Black. While none of them are perfect (who is?!), they've got strong self-esteem, and are grounded, compassionate, self-aware people. They give me hope.

Earlier in this chapter, when I wrote that I hadn't experienced racism as an adult other than when that drunk woman called me the N-word, I should have been more specific. I hadn't experienced racism from any other *white* people. But I have experienced plenty of *colorism*, and it was incredibly painful. Colorism is when someone with dark skin is discriminated against by people in the same ethnic or racial group.

When we got together to film the *Basketball Wives* reunion show in November 2020, Evelyn Lozada was in fine form. I love her to death and she's one of my best friends, but she's a hothead and says pretty much whatever she's thinking. That's what makes her so entertaining. Well, she got into an argument with one of the other cast members who has very dark skin. Evelyn said something nasty about the other woman's appearance, and the insults went back and forth until she called the other woman downright ugly. When the episode aired, millions of viewers decided that Evelyn had said what she said because of the other woman's dark skin.

I didn't jump in right away because I didn't think it was a big deal, and that was a mistake. Immediately after the episode ran, the media and Twitter accused Evelyn of being a colorist, and they declared me guilty by association. Evelyn never said a word about the other woman's color; the accusations of colorism were unfair and ridiculous. The whole thing was a misunderstanding and completely blown out of proportion. But the online mob had tasted blood, and explanations didn't matter. I spent months dealing with accusations and getting calls from magazines like *Essence*, which ran critical stories saying that I hadn't pushed back forcefully enough against Evelyn's supposed colorism. It was horrible. According to the internet, I only had friends who were light-skinned, pretty women. Total BS.

Colorism and intra-ethnic prejudice are real, and not just in the Black community. Human beings seem wired to look for any reason to feel superior to other human beings. For instance, right now, it's not popular to be a light-skinned Black person in this country. Not that long ago, everybody wanted light skin because they thought it came with privilege. But now, because of forces like Black Lives Matter and interest in diversity and equity, light-skinned Black people supposedly don't understand what dark-skinned Black people go through. We're not as *real*. It's *reverse* colorism.

A while back a Black comedian posted an online video tribute to Black women. It featured Black male celebrities talking about how much they love Black women. But in this video, which was maybe three minutes long, every woman was dark-skinned. One of my girlfriends (who's light-skinned like me) put the video in the group text we all share. She wrote, "Did you guys notice that there was not one light-skinned Black woman in that video?" I replied, "Yeah, it's not very popular to be a light-skinned Black woman right now."

It's important to push back against racism where and when you can, but sometimes the best way to deal with the daily, casual racism in our society is to rise above it. Here's an example of what I mean. A few winters ago I took Myles and Shaqir to Park City, Utah, so we could go skiing. If you know anything about Utah, you know it's very beautiful and very, *very* white. Well, Park City is even whiter than that. Everywhere we went, we were the only Black people. People were staring at us as they skied down the slopes, to the point where I worried someone was going to end up skiing into a tree.

This "passive" racism became less passive and more obvious when we went to dinner at Ruth's Chris Steak House. As soon as we walked in the door, everyone was staring at us. Shaqir, who at the time was not quite eighteen, whispered, "Mom, we're the only Black people in here for sure. Every table is looking at us." It was true. Kids were turning around in their seats and looking over the backs of their booths to watch us, and their parents weren't stopping them because they were doing the same thing! Everywhere we went during that week, it was the same.

My sons handled it differently. Myles is a very intense Taurus, brutally honest and passionate about whatever the conversation is. He's going to call it like it is. We would go out to dinner and the older white people would turn their noses up, and I remember thinking, *If some white lady grabs her purse when Myles walks by, it's going to be on.* Passive racism provokes you because there's nothing to fight. You can't punch stupidity.

Sometimes, when all else fails, the best way to deal with ignorant, racist people can be to laugh at them. My family loves to ski, and we almost always go to Park City. When we do, we usually have at least one person with us who's never skied before, so we'll hire this white ski instructor based there. He's awesome, and he'll meet up with us and teach the newbies.

Let me tell you, the looks and double takes that this man gets from all the white skiers as we all wait together on the lift line, laughing and joking, are *hilarious*. When he's taking a break and not with us for a few minutes, some white person will inevitably pull him aside and ask, "Where are you from?"

He'll answer, "Park City," which is true.

The other person always huffs something like, "Well *they're* not." Meaning me and my family. This poor instructor had never experienced this sort of thing before, and he was angry about it at first, but now he finds it funny. After our fourth trip up, he finally said to me, with total sincerity, "You know, I've lived here for seven years, and I really think a lot of these people are racist."

You think? Oh my God, we laughed so hard at that.

On another trip, we were in an Uber, riding to a place where we could go ax throwing, and Myles (who is a straight shooter) said to the driver, "Dude, this is a pretty white city. Is there a lot of meth going on here?" I practically came unglued, but the guy said, "Actually, it's so bad. Meth is really taking over the city of Salt Lake."

Myles nodded and said, "I totally can see that. Look at these guys," pointing out some sketchy-looking white guys on the street. "It's really white, but it's that methy kind of white." How can you not laugh at that?

CHAPTER 4

THE LIGHT AT THE END
OF THE TUNNEL

I've said that I'm a vastly different woman today than I was twenty years ago, but that's not much of a revelation. None of us is the same person we were in college, or when we first got married—at least I hope not. We go through challenges and hardships and come out the other side having learned some important lessons that have hopefully changed us for the better, with a stronger sense of who we are and what we're meant to do. The Shaunie I am today has no problem staring down challenges and dealing with them. But I wasn't always that way. For years I lied to myself and believed those lies. I tolerated things no woman should tolerate.

Of course, I'm talking about infidelity. Everything I went through around the failure of my marriage changed me and shaped me into the woman I am today. It was hell, some of it self-inflicted, but I wouldn't have accomplished what I have without it.

Before Shaquille, I had never dated a professional athlete. But even before I became part of the NBA family as a girlfriend, I had heard the rumors about players cheating on their wives and figured at least some of them were true. Word on the street was that cheating was rampant in the league, with some players having a mistress in practically every city. Being an NBA wife or serious girlfriend meant accepting that while your man was on the road, he was probably spending his off-court time in bed with other ladies while you looked the other way because of the wealth and lifestyle it afforded you. It was an unspoken agreement that none of the women talked about.

Well, I've never been dazzled by wealth and celebrity. Growing up, I was raised to look at substance, not style. So, while I didn't think Shaquille was perfect, I chose to play the "boys will be boys" game when it came to what he may or may not be doing on the road. We weren't married, and I figured he was going to make some mistakes, but we would get through it.

The first experience that forced me to confront the questionable morality that existed in the NBA came when I traveled with the Lakers to Charlotte, North Carolina, in 2000 for a game against the Hornets. Shaquille and I were still just dating, but I had already given birth to Shareef, so it was widely known that I was his serious, long-term girlfriend. The team traveled on its own plane, so I, along with the other wives and girlfriends, arrived at the hotel separately, after the Lakers had checked in. I walked into the lobby, where at least ten or twelve young, attractive women were milling about, dressed like they were going out to a club and looking to take home a man: short, tight dresses, styled hair, stiletto heels, lots of makeup, the works.

I called Shaquille to get our room number, and he told me he had run to the store and would be right back, and that I should wait for him downstairs. I sat in the lobby as instructed, watching player after player come down, put his arm around one of those hot young women, and get back in the elevator. It happened repeatedly, and it didn't take much imagination to figure out what would happen when those players and those girls got upstairs.

Today, I would have figured out what was happening in about ten seconds, but back in those more innocent days, it took me a little longer. As I sat there and waited, it hit me: All these women were there to hook up with the players! I wasn't dressed like them because I wasn't one of them. But I was still taken aback. Was this the club I was joining?

I didn't know most of the Lakers players personally yet. But I saw at least one guy who I knew was married come down and go right up to one of the girls, who immediately wrapped herself around him like a cat. That was my real-life introduction to one of the realities of NBA life on the road: the temptation to cheat. Wherever there were players, there were women. I had no idea how many guys were taking advantage of this "opportunity," but my impression was that many players were unfaithful to their wives and girlfriends. What I found disturbing was that no one would talk about any of it. Even when it was obvious that some players were fooling around, the wives and girlfriends back home would pretend everything was fine. It was a culture of denial, and for years I was a willing participant.

The second time I encountered something that raised my suspicions, I literally came face to face with it. Before we were married, I was at a game at the Staples Center with Shareef, who was only nine months old, and Myles, who was three. I left the suite to get the kids something to eat and while I was standing in line, holding Myles's hand, a woman walked up to me with two of her girlfriends and started screaming in my face—making a scene, calling me a bitch, and saying things like, "You think having a baby is going to get you in there? You're trying to trap him. That's *my* man!"

What do you do in a situation like that? I had no idea what was going on, but I knew this crazy, screaming woman was standing so close to me that her nose was almost touching mine. Meanwhile, her girlfriends were at her back, and there I was alone, with my baby and my toddler. We would have ended up in a brawl if some of Shaquille's friends at a nearby table hadn't come over and broken things up.

The crazy woman and her pack of friends retreated, and I began falling into what would become a lengthy pattern of denial. I told myself, *She's crazy. She just wants what I have. There's nothing going on.* I never mentioned the incident to Shaquille. It was easier for me to simply pretend it didn't happen.

A few years later, we were married and had two more children, and life was dazzling. A few years earlier, I'd been a single mom with a mid-level job at Fox. And now here I was, going to Eddie Murphy's house for birthday parties. The travel and media attention that came with being an NBA wife never really won me over, but I won't say I didn't enjoy the mansions, the cars, and the expensive vacations to anywhere we wanted to go. But as time went by, I started seeing cracks in the facade of our marriage that became harder and harder to ignore.

In 2005, the NBA All-Star Game was in Denver, and I attended the All-Star Weekend with some of my girlfriends. Shaquille was playing with the Miami Heat then. I arrived at the hotel where the team usually stayed when they were in town. The check-in clerk said, "Oh, Ms. O'Neal, you left your scarf and gloves here last time. I'll get them for you." Before I could say anything, he brought out a scarf and gloves that were not mine. I had never been to this hotel before.

To avoid an embarrassing moment for both of us, I acted like I was whoever this guy thought I was. He said something like, "You grew your hair out." I don't remember what my hair was like back then, but it was obviously the opposite of whatever he had seen the last time he thought I had been there. Then he said, "Can I get you your tea?" I don't drink tea. Whoever this front-desk clerk thought I was, she had clearly been to the hotel multiple times, posing as "Ms. O'Neal," because she had a standard order. I was now seething with anger, but I played along, gathering as much information as I could.

We drove to the dunk contest, and I refused to get out of the car. We fought the entire weekend. It was the most humiliating weekend of my life because I was complicit in my own humiliation. I knew what was happening, but I didn't want to do anything about it.

One of our biggest blowups came some months later. I headed to Mimi's school for her playgroup while Shaquille headed to practice. While the kids were playing, I got out my BlackBerry (yes, it was *that* long ago) to check it, and I realized Shaquille and I had accidentally switched phones. But when I looked at the contents of his, I saw evidence I simply could not deny.

I felt sick. While we had had problems before, there was no coming back from this. I could no longer turn a blind eye, pretend it wasn't happening, and just focus on "the good things." And while a part of me had known all along that this was happening, I was still devastated, because I could no longer tell myself comforting lies to avoid the truth. I had no choice but to face my role in enabling what was going on.

We fought horribly. Then we went days without speaking, which was somehow worse. Shaquille promised that it would never happen again, and became so sad that it actually hurt me to see him that way. Finally, things got so bad that my parents flew down to Miami and laid down the law: *Settle this. You cannot continue to be at war in front of your children.* I'm not proud of this, but I ended up giving him another chance.

I don't know why I stayed. That's the truth. Some of my critics will insist that I stayed in the marriage for the lifestyle—that I didn't want to give up the money, fancy cars, luxury vacations, and all the rest. But it's just not true. I was raised to value family above everything else, and my instinct was to keep my family intact at all costs, even the cost of my own happiness. Inertia also played a part. Was I really prepared to tear apart our home, pull my children out of their schools, spend God knows how long fighting with lawyers, and build a new life while explaining everything to my family and friends? Right then, the answer was no.

Looking back from the vantage point of the woman I am today, it's hard for me to believe I stayed for as long as I did. Early on I really thought I loved my husband, and I desperately loved my family and wanted to try and protect and save it. I saw the other women as the enemy, and I would say things to myself like, *I won't let them win. They're trying to break us up. They're doing this on purpose!* To me, these unknown women were putting a lot of effort into trying to ruin our relationship.

For a long time I failed to see how unhappy I was and how low my overall energy was. I was just trying to keep all the balls in the air, look after the kids, and make sure they were going down the right path.

Eventually, my relationships with my friends and family began to suffer because I refused to admit the truth. I probably only had one good friend at the time—Alicia, who I've known forever. She was very supportive and would listen to me cry, cuss, and fuss. She would say, "If you leave, tell me when you need me to get the boxes and tape. I'm rolling because I love you."

But that was it. None of my other friends were seeing what I was seeing, and I never shared how I felt or what was going on. But even if they had put the clues together, what were they supposed to do? No woman wants to be the one who blows up a friendship because she decides to say, "Your husband's cheating." So my friends were between a rock and a hard place. They could speak up, and maybe ruin my marriage and lose me as their friend, or say nothing and have everything be tense and awkward.

Everybody chose to say nothing, and I played along like life was great. But it was awful. During that time I was not the best friend I could be, or the best sister, or the best daughter. I didn't even realize how unhappy I was until my sister, Cori, came to town, and we got into a huge fight after she accused me of being miserable. My response? "Look at my car! Look at my house! Look at the things I get to do. How can I be miserable?" But I was. I just didn't want to admit it.

Now, you need to understand that Cori and I never fought. *Ever.* Growing up, we didn't even have minor arguments. We're six years apart, and I think our biggest disagreement to that point had been a "Can I have my jeans back?" kind of thing. She's so even-tempered that it's hard to even get her to argue. But there we were, yelling at each other. Our fight got so heated that I ended up kicking her out of my house, shouting, "Get out!" After that, we didn't speak for a month.

I wasn't sure who I was anymore. It took that moment, with Cori, for me to start recognizing the horrible way I was treating people, talking to people, and cutting people out of my life who didn't deserve it. I hated who I was becoming, and I didn't want to deal with anyone who would call me out on it. In that moment, I hated everything about my life other than my children.

Soon after, I fell into a deep depression. For months I spent the majority of my day in bed feeling sad and alone. I wasn't being much of a mom, either. Most days I would get up, take the kids to school, come back, shower, and then get back in bed for the rest of the day. Sometimes my mom would go and pick the kids up after school because I just didn't have the energy or motivation to get out of bed. More than once I woke up looking at the morning sun and wishing night would come again so I could go back to sleep. I would think, *Oh my God, I have twelve hours of sunlight to push through.*

I know. It was messed up. That's not the Shaunie you thought you knew. That's not the Shaunie I thought I knew, either. Frankly, I hardly recognized myself. That was, without a doubt, the darkest time of my entire life. That was rock bottom. I had gotten so used to living this way that I couldn't imagine living any other way. My depression and sadness got so bad that in 2007, when Shareef was in second grade at Miami Country Day School, his teacher called me one day and said, "This is the second day Shareef has asked me to call his grandmother to come and get him because he needs to go check on his mom. What's going on?"

Oh my God. My kids could see something was very wrong with me and it scared them. Of course it did! I needed to find the strength to move past my depression and denial and pull myself and our family together.

Finally, feeling like my back was against the wall, with no other options in sight, I suggested that Shaquille and I separate. To my surprise, he didn't seem that upset. He told me he didn't think he was cut out for married life. The responsibilities were just too overwhelming. Me, I felt guilty about depriving my children of a two-parent home (even a dysfunctional one), but I knew nothing would change unless I made a change. Knowing that meant that I simply could not stay.

I'm not proud of the fact that I spent so many years in denial. It just shows how easy it is to slip into patterns and become comfortable with them, even when they're toxic. For a long time I thought, *I have to stay to make my kids happy.* Ironically, staying was actually making my kids *unhappy*, but in the moment, while it was happening, I couldn't see that. It's hard to be self-aware when your mind is clouded with all the daily stuff of life. You can forget to step back and take a good look at yourself and the life you're leading.

I wish more than anything that toward the middle and end of my marriage I'd had the ability to self-reflect. *Am I being me right now? Am I happy with the face I'm showing everybody else right now?* But I was barely functioning, just going through the motions, not even knowing that I was as unhappy as I was, and not giving my kids, family, or friends the real me. Nobody was calling me on it either.

Still, while it was an incredibly tough time in my life, I have no regrets. I wouldn't be the woman I am today if I hadn't gone through all that—the depression and darkness, the rage and frustration, the lies, and the self-deception. That experience led me to become fiercely independent about my income, my career, and my identity. Right then and there I decided that no man would ever define me again, and no man has.

CHAPTER 5

THE END OF MY MARRIAGE
WAS THE BEGINNING

One of the ways in which I have grown since my early days as a young mother and wife is that I don't fear what might happen if a relationship ends. Like many women, one of the reasons I didn't leave my marriage sooner is that I worried about being able to financially support myself and my children. My husband had provided everything, and I think my self-reliance muscles had gotten a little soft.

That's unhealthy for any woman. Too often we rely on our romantic relationships to define us but also to rescue us. Some women talk about marriage like it's going to change who they are—like "I do" is a magical spell that's going to make them a different person. Their goal is to find a man, get married . . . and then what? If there's no answer to "then what?" we can end up with marriage and motherhood becoming our entire identity. That's what had happened to me as I contemplated ending my marriage.

Shaquille and I had separated while he was playing for the Miami Heat, and when he was traded to the Phoenix Suns, things didn't get any better. When we decided to try to get back together, the result was a disaster.

In June 2009, he was traded to the Cleveland Cavaliers. School had ended and the kids and I had already moved down to the house in Orlando, which was fun for them because there was so much to do. But when we got there, Shaquille asked us to stay in Orlando while he rented a house in Cleveland and got settled. After that, he said, I could decide if I wanted to move to Cleveland full time (which I didn't want to do) or just travel back and forth. This was very strange. He had never been traded to a team and then left us behind. He had never said, "I'm going to go play the season and you guys stay here and just come and visit." It was like he was giving up on our marriage. But I agreed, so off he went to Cleveland.

Things were quiet for a few months, and then they started happening quickly. I took the kids to Cleveland to attend the opening game of the Cavaliers' season on October 27, 2009. I arrived at the house Shaquille had rented and was greeted by the housekeeper . . . who led me and the kids to the guest rooms. She kept saying, "The missus will be back soon," and immediately I knew what was going on. This very kind housekeeper had met some other woman and been told that she was the lady of the house. I'm pretty sure she thought I was either a family member traveling with her kids or the nanny. I had come full circle; now *I* was Mary Poppins!

A few years earlier, something like this would have enraged me. But now it didn't even bother me. I didn't care anymore. I had checked out of the marriage. So, I just smiled, took my things into the guest room without another word, and settled in. We went to the opening game, and I had our flights changed so we could leave the next morning instead of staying for a while. There was no conversation about what had happened with the housekeeper.

When the kids and I got home on October 28, I called Shaquille and told him we were not moving to Cleveland. A few days after that, a gentleman who worked for us as an IT professional approached me. He gave me a CD on which he had burned copies of all the evidence I needed to prove to myself that my marriage was irrevocably broken.

That was it. That was the final straw. I hated my house. I hated the cars. I hated my bed. I hated my life. I hated myself for tolerating all of it for so long. I had finally reached my breaking point, and I had to do something.

By 2009 Shaquille and I had been together for ten years and married for nearly seven, and I was ready to file for divorce. But there was a problem. If Shaquille learned about what I had in mind, we would end up fighting nonstop. My sanity couldn't handle that. Also, if anyone in the press or on social media caught on to what was happening, our problems would quickly become a very public spectacle. I didn't want to embarrass the kids, and I certainly didn't want to attract any attention to myself. So, I kept quiet and made my plans, thinking about when and where we would go as soon as I filed. I wanted to file and begin moving toward the next stage of my life.

I didn't tell the kids anything right away. I packed up clothes and things and told them we were going to Los Angeles. That wasn't anything new, because we went to L.A. all the time. The one person I couldn't keep my plans a secret from was my mother. I had to let her know, because I needed her support to take this big, painful step. It was early November, and she was staying with us in Orlando. After looking at what was on that CD the IT guy handed me, I immediately went down the hall to my mom's room and showed her the text messages and emails that were on it. Her only response was "Oh my God." She knew the girl from one of the text messages, and she sat on the edge of the bed in shock.

Here's something about my mom. She might be prim and proper, but when it comes to her children, she will turn into a whole different person who you don't want to mess with. When I told her what was going on, I was as angry as I've ever been in my life. I never, ever curse around my mother, but I said to her, "Mom, as soon as I see her I'm going to whoop her ass."

My mom's response startled me. She said, "As you should!" My God, how can you not love that? That's who Mary is. She might quote you scripture, but if you mess with one of her kids, she's going to put her sneakers on and be ready to lay you out. She's my ride or die.

Mom and I didn't roll up on this woman and lay a beatdown on her, but I did call her with my mom in the room. I was in full confrontation mode; if I was going to do this, I was going to *do this*.

I got her on the phone and said, "I just saw all your text messages to my husband." I was very specific, and she was stammering, "Oh no, this has got to be a mistake. Just let me explain."

"When I see you, I'm going to whoop your ass," I said. Meanwhile, my mother was in the background saying the same thing. The tiger mama was out of her cage! I hung up and said, "I'm out of here. I'm going to pack up." That was the one time I can remember that she didn't give me advice. She didn't say, "Yes you should," and she didn't say, "Oh, no, honey, don't do it." She simply said, "Just tell me what to do. Tell me what you need from me. I'm not going to give you any problems."

Deep down, I think she would've liked me to stay in my marriage, like she did with my father. But I didn't want to be an angry woman for the rest of my life. Mom's attitude was (and still is), "They're men. They're going to mess up all the time. Get over it and move on." But I can't do that. Messing up is when you burn dinner or wash a piece of my clothing that's dry clean only. If I had stayed, I would have chosen misery and denial. I value myself more than that.

I want to be affectionate with my husband and not feel dirty. I don't want to feel like he's dirty. When he comes in the door, I want to give him a kiss and cuddle with him and not ask myself, *Has he done this with three other women today behind my back?* I don't want that burden for the rest of my life.

My mother stayed with my father after his infidelity, but she never forgave him for what he did. Because of that, from the time I was five or six, I never saw affection between my parents. Not a hug. Not a kiss. When we were adults, my sister and I went to our mom and asked her if she was still so angry at him all the time, why didn't she just leave? We loved our dad, but we could see he wasn't a very good husband. But she wouldn't even consider it. In her mind, when you got married, that was it. So, she stayed. She wouldn't leave, and she wouldn't forgive, and until the day he died, that's how she remained.

I didn't want to live like that. What's the point of staying married for fifty years if there's no love? If there's no love or trust, why are you together? There's no virtue in staying together because you think you're supposed to. I wanted more out of my life than that.

My mom saw that I was of a different mind than she was, and she respected that. Her position was, "I'm going to sit over here and be quiet. You tell me what you need me to pack and what you need me to do." She had become my 2 a.m. friend, the person you can call at two in the morning to help you bury a dead body. They'll not only show up, but they'll show up with a shovel and *two* pairs of gloves.

On November 10, 2009, I filed to dissolve my marriage. On the same day, I flew with my children to Los Angeles to where my parents and family were. I wanted to go home.

Despite my lawyers' advice, I didn't want anything from Shaquille. I just wanted out. I kept telling him, "You don't have to give me anything, just take care of the kids." Of course, he was legally bound to take financial responsibility for the kids, which he did, but outside of that, all I wanted was my car, which was in my name. The only other thing I wanted was peace of mind. I was hungry for it. I just wanted to live honestly and without lies or self-deception.

After the kids and I left, we landed at my parents' house in L.A., the six of us sleeping in two rooms with no idea what to do next. I had a little bit of money put aside in the bank from my "allowance," but it wasn't enough to rent a house big enough for me and five children. I went to my parents' house because I didn't want to take the kids to a hotel to stay for God knows how long. I shipped my car and all our things from Florida, so what money I had was going into getting us where we needed to be. I knew I would have to wait for the divorce to be final to get money to look after the kids, so I needed my family. They were my only option.

My mom and dad responded exactly how I needed them to. When I asked if we could land at their place while I figured things out, they just said, "Absolutely. Come here. We don't want you in a hotel or moving around from place to place. Come stay here until you get stable." Sometimes, no matter how old you are, you just need to go home to where love doesn't come with strings attached.

One of the beautiful things about being at my parents' house was that nobody, besides my family and my close girlfriends, knew where we were. (I had to let Shaquille know where we were, of course.) But we had quietly disappeared, and I had the time and space to gather my thoughts. Unfortunately, my thoughts were screaming, *What the hell have I done with my life? How did I end up here?*

I was terrified, because I didn't know how this divorce was going to go. My kids, on the other hand, were doing great. At first they thought it was all a fun adventure, because they were sleeping over at their grandparents' house, where they got tons of love and everything was wonderful. That lasted for a few days. Then I started enrolling them in school and things like that, and they started to wonder what was going on. But I never got the sense that they were scared or homesick.

They were an adaptable bunch. We had moved so many times over the years—from L.A. to Miami to Phoenix to Orlando—and they had been in so many different schools that moving didn't throw them. Especially for Myles, Shareef, and Amirah, who had been there for all the moves, this was more like, "We're moving back to L.A.? Cool." They had friends and family there, so they were good. They didn't ask a lot of questions, which was a blessing, because I didn't really want to answer the questions they would have asked. I limited it to, "We're going to live here in Los Angeles, your dad's going to live in Cleveland,

and everything's going to be fine." That was just the way it was, and they rolled with it.

Finally, a few months later, I knew I had to level with them. I sat the kids down and said, "We are in Los Angeles because your dad and I are no longer going to be together. We're not going to be married anymore." None of them seemed upset. There were no tears. Some of them asked why we were splitting up, but nobody was particularly sad. I was so alarmed by their calm demeanor that I started taking them to a therapist.

I told him, "Something's wrong because they don't seem to care that their dad and I are divorcing." At first he agreed that it wasn't normal, but after he talked with the kids, he said, "They're fine. They're just kind of disconnected from their father. What I get from them is, 'Oh, we won't see him every day? Okay. Business as usual.' "

My children were fine. People ask me, "How did you get five kids through a divorce?" It was the fact that they had never had the foundation of a happy home, so they weren't losing one. All the guilt I had been feeling about breaking up this traditional two-parent family had been misplaced. There was no residue of divorce for them, which was such a blessing.

Of course, after we left I totally overcompensated. I overdid it with affection and distractions because I had always heard that that's what you were supposed to do when you got a divorce. You had to make up for the hurt you were putting your kids through. I was doing all of that and not seeing that they were okay. They were—and are—so smart, so sophisticated, and so brave. I don't know how they got that way but I'm grateful.

My overcompensation made us closer in those uncertain first few months. We bonded even more deeply; we were just there for each other. I was a better version of myself, and our lives changed completely. Everybody's happiness started to get turned up to another level.

Unfortunately, as hard as I tried to keep the end of our marriage from turning into a public nightmare, the internet had other ideas. When Shaquille and I announced that we were getting a divorce, people started saying horrible things about me on social media. Rumor had it that *he* was divorcing *me*, when in reality I had been the one who filed. In no time, a story appeared claiming that Shaquille was divorcing me because I was having an affair with my personal trainer. I didn't even work out back then, so there was no trainer to have an affair with! Naturally, the story went viral.

I was disgusted. But the next accusation was even worse: He was divorcing me because I had been stealing money from him—with my *mother* as my accomplice! Remember Robin Givens, who used to be married to Mike Tyson? When the marriage went south, Tyson accused Robin and her mother of stealing money from him. Now the vultures on social media were doing the same thing to me. Supposedly my mother and I were secretly funneling money from Shaquille—and, of course, the mob ran with it.

I can defend myself without a problem, but to attack my mom, who has no idea how Facebook or Twitter even work, was inexcusable. But the story was everywhere. There was nothing I could do to stop it. Unbelievably, it's still around today. In 2023, when I was putting the final changes to this book, I googled "Shaunie O'Neal affair with trainer" and found an article on some second-rate sports news website saying that I had cheated on Shaquille with not one but *three* men. I certainly got around, didn't I? Appalling.

While all this was happening, Wendy Williams asked me to appear on her show. On December 14, 2009, I sat down for an interview, hoping I could get the truth out there. Wendy was truly kind to me and said, "Listen, I'm going to let you talk. There's a lot of things out there about what you did or didn't do." I was able to say, "It's a lie. I never had an affair. I don't even have a trainer. I haven't taken any money."

Yeah, you've probably already guessed what happened. I was wasting my breath. Social media blew up. Everyone said, "She's lying. Of course she's going to say that." I had become the conniving, greedy bitch who was betraying a beloved American sports hero. Going on the show had been a waste of time. My voice didn't matter. I wasn't ever going to get control of the story. Nobody was going to listen to me, because they were having too much fun (and getting lots of followers and retweets) taking me down.

I had to live with the embarrassment and hope that over time people would slowly forget about it. I had to endure going to the stylist or the store and overhear people saying vicious, false things about me behind my back. Finally, about a month before Keion and I got married, Shaquille was a guest on a podcast where he confessed that I was the best thing that ever happened to him, had been the perfect wife and mom, and that it had been his fault that our marriage ended. It was a nice gesture, even if it came twelve years too late, and I appreciated it.

.   .   .

When the kids and I left Orlando, the most obvious change was in our standard of living. We went from ostentatious luxury to a modest and much more simple way of life. But that was okay with me. I didn't want my children to ever feel entitled to any of the things we had when we were living on an NBA salary. That said, I worried about the outcome of the divorce financially. I worried where my kids and I would end up.

I went back and forth with my attorneys endlessly because Shaquille's attorneys kept coming back with conditions and demands, and my lawyer didn't seem to be pushing back very hard, saying things like, "According to the law, you can only do this, and you can only do that." Thank you, but I want to know how you're going to fight for my kids! In that moment I didn't have much fight left in me, which is why I needed my lawyer to have my back.

Amid all this worry and stress, I found a new determination to work toward a lifestyle my kids could relate to. Not because I wanted to spoil them, but because they hadn't known anything else. It wasn't fair of me to take them away from the life they had known and drop them into a new life and environment they'd never experienced. None of this was their fault. At that moment I couldn't imagine ever having Shaquille's wealth (little did I know I would soon be on my way to getting as close as possible), but I would do everything I could do to keep life from seeming so drastically different. That was the very beginning of the mindset that would lead me to create *Basketball Wives*.

At the same time—and this seems strange to say because the conflict surrounding the divorce was so ugly—I felt . . . liberated. I had finally stopped lying to myself and rationalizing. I wasn't the victim anymore. I felt stronger in escaping from the emotionally sunken place I had been in. I can't blame Shaquille for my prior emotional state. That was on me. I had made so many excuses and compromises that I barely knew who I was anymore. Now, I was beginning to remember. I had filed for divorce. I started to feel like whatever was coming my way, let's go. Bring it on.

We lived at my mom and dad's house for two months as I got my footing as a single working mom. The kids started school and we got into a semi-routine. We ended up being able to move out because I asked my attorney if I could get some money prior to the finalization of the divorce so we could get a place of our own. My parents loved having all their grandkids under one roof, but things were pretty crowded. I wanted the kids to be settled as soon as possible. That was the only time I asked for anything during that process, and Shaquille graciously agreed. We moved out of my parents' house and into a rental home, and a few months later, when the divorce was finalized in 2010, I began getting child support payments, which was a huge help.

Years later, I'm proud to say that Shaquille and I settled into a sort of peaceful coexistence centered around the kids. It was like they were the neutral ground where we could meet and negotiate in good faith. I would ask him for things like, "Hey, I'm trying to get the kids into this school and I'm having a hard time. Could you make a call or have your people make a call?" No problem. In fact, today our relationship is amicable and reasonable.

A few years after our divorce we had a very honest and satisfying conversation. He talked about his infidelity and said, "What's crazy is that cheating was an ego boost. It wasn't even about the girl. It wasn't about me falling for someone or having feelings for her. It was about getting away with it." It was, he said, about getting another girl, and then another, and then another. It was about conquest. He knew that in no way justified his behavior, but I appreciated his honesty about it.

With the kids mostly grown and out of the house, Shaquille and I don't have to communicate all that often, so things are much better. He wasn't happy when I got engaged to Keion. He told me he felt like I should have called and let him know I was engaged before it went public. Why would I do that? But eventually he came around. He's met Keion, and he's respectful. We are doing very well again. We can be parents to our kids, cordial to each other, and live our own lives. I call that a win.

One more thing happened to help me move on from my broken marriage, and it was as unusual as it was unexpected. It was early 2010, and our divorce process had become painfully public. I was walking into the Radio Shack in Ladera Heights, where my parents lived, to get a phone charger. Walking through the parking lot, this Mercedes-Benz caught my attention, but I dismissed it. In the store, I was looking at chargers when this woman walked up to me and said, "You're Shaunie, right?"

I said yes. But I wanted to hide. This was when all the lies were circulating around our divorce—how I had cheated on Shaquille, how I had stolen money, and so on. It felt like everybody in the world was judging me, talking about me, had an opinion about me, or was lying about me. The kids and I were still staying at my parents' house, and I pretty much stayed inside all the time except for taking my kids to school and picking them up. I had gone out for fifteen minutes and now I was thinking, *Great, here's a woman who's probably about to talk shit about me.*

She introduced herself, and her name rang a bell. She said, "I just want to say I'm sorry. I was one of your soon-to-be ex-husband's mistresses, and I was well aware of you and the kids and all that. Still, I remained that person in his life for quite some time." I noticed that she wore big diamond stud earrings, which was a strange thing to notice at that moment.

She went on. "I'm in a relationship now and it's serious. I understand what it would feel like if someone like me was to be part of that relationship. So I just want to say I'm sorry. I needed to get that off my conscience because I'm entering this new phase in my life where I'm just trying to right my wrongs." I just stood there, stunned, and suddenly I knew instinctively that he had bought the diamond studs she was wearing. She had stopped messing around with him, but she still had the stuff.

Then this woman said something I'll never forget. "It wasn't you," she began. "Men . . . sometimes the pressure makes them seek an outlet. When he would come to see me, he got a release. He didn't have to face bills, kids, or responsibility. He didn't have to face any of what real life holds for him when he goes home. He could come to me and I could do cartwheels when he came in the door—make him feel missed and celebrate him, because it's for a limited time. Then he goes home to you and he's got kids, bills, responsibilities, things he has to show up for, and people he has to show up for. Just know that it wasn't you. It never is. In some cases, maybe a woman pushes a man away, but I know for a fact it wasn't you."

This woman really said all that to me, standing there in Radio Shack. I still couldn't speak when she said, "I just needed to say that," and walked away. I just stood there, my jaw on the floor. What the hell was I supposed to say to that? "Thank you" didn't seem appropriate. It wasn't until I replayed the conversation over and over for a couple of years that I was able to see that she was right. It wasn't about me. She represented no responsibilities, worries, issues, or complaints. I represented husband duties, father duties, and man-of-the-house duties. It was never about me. She was wrong about one thing, though. Not all men respond to pressure that way. Some men step up.

My divorce didn't answer all my questions or silence all my self-doubt. It lifted a huge weight, which was a blessing. But I still struggled with my self-confidence. I worried that I was failing my children. Sometimes I was terrified I was making a huge mistake. But eventually things stabilized. We started to build a new life in Los Angeles. I was home. I was free.

CHAPTER 6

BLACK WIVES MATTER

One of my greatest sources of pride is creating *Basketball Wives* and producing the show for more than ten years. It's changed my life and become a franchise that's led to spin-offs like *Football Wives* and *Shaunie's Home Court*, and as I write this, we're developing a version of *Basketball Wives* that takes place in Orlando. But the idea for the original show, and my passion to make it happen, came out of a darker place: my fear that I would not be able to be financially independent after my divorce.

I wasn't a complete stranger to the world of television. Years earlier, when Shaquille was still playing for the Lakers, he had an amazing house in Orlando that practically came with its own amusement park. One summer, *MTV Cribs* came to the house to film a segment, and I played the designated role of hostess and tour guide. When we finished filming, one of the producers said to me, "Have you ever thought about doing TV? You speak so well, and you have this great personality and presence." I didn't really think much of this at the time, but fast-forward to a Lakers game, and one of the executive producers of *Access Hollywood* asked to meet with me.

He had heard about me from the MTV people, and he had an idea. Would I be interested in hosting some of *Access Hollywood*'s sports segments, even talking to athletes? I couldn't say yes fast enough. That's how my TV career really got started. Then Jeanie Buss, daughter of then Lakers owner Jerry Buss and who now has controlling interest in the team, approached me. She had started a Lakers halftime talk show on Fox and asked me to cohost with her. We did that for a little while, and I loved it. That was the beginning of a new identity, a new, better version of Shaunie.

I needed that version, because while I was ready to move on with my life after the divorce, I hadn't been financially independent in years. Before marrying, I had a full-time job and took care of myself on a paycheck-to-paycheck basis. I wasn't broke, but I wasn't living the high life. I had a one-bedroom apartment and drove a Honda Accord. It wasn't glamorous, but I was working and figuring it all out.

When I got married in my late twenties, I was very well taken care of. I started to think, *Well, this is the way life is. I'll want for nothing and get to be a wife and mother.* I thoroughly enjoy being a mom, as you know, and I spent years being so busy with my children that I didn't have time to think about my career aspirations. But I had lots of entrepreneurial ideas. When I had a spare moment, I would go as far as writing out business plans, but I'd get no support at home for my ideas. I would put those plans in a drawer and move on, but I never forgot about them. I knew that someday I would want to be more than a mother, and as time went on, my kids grew up, and my marriage went south, that desire got stronger.

As I thought about what my life would look like after a divorce, I regretted not forcing the issue, because I realized that every dime I had had come from my marriage. It was a humiliating, discouraging feeling. I felt helpless. I did not have anything that was mine. I didn't even have a legacy to leave my kids.

I thought, *I will not allow this to be my life. I will never be financially dependent on anyone again.* I've seen women who seem content to depend on their husbands for everything. They spend their days shopping and going to the salon, handing their children off to a nanny. Not me. I would never be one of those women at Saks Fifth Avenue, rolling up to the salesclerk with $10,000 worth of clothes and accessories and saying, "He's got it," as my man pulls out his AmEx Platinum card. No thank you. I had to become self-sufficient, but how?

Since 2008, when we had been living in Phoenix, I had been toying with the idea of a reality show based on the wives of NBA players. *Keeping up with the Kardashians* had started in 2007 and had become a monster hit, and reality television was becoming incredibly popular. People were always asking me what life was like being in the NBA and hanging around with the other players' wives. They would ask me things like, "What do you ladies do?" "Do you all hang out? Do you shop together?" "What are some glamorous things you get to go to?" and "Do you fly all over the place together?" Obviously, people thought my life was much more exciting than it actually was, but that gave me an idea. In 2009, knowing that I was going to be leaving my marriage and looking for a way to establish a new identity and support myself and my children, I decided to see if I could put a TV show together.

I had some experience as a television host, but I didn't know anything about TV production or being an executive producer. However, I did have one thing going for me. After all those years in the NBA, living in Los Angeles, Miami, and Phoenix and traveling all over the country, I knew a lot of NBA wives and girlfriends who were both terrific ladies *and* larger-than-life characters. I called some of those women and said, "If I was able to put a reality TV show together, would you be interested in being on it?" Some said no right away. The first one to say yes was Evelyn Lozada.

Evelyn was the first person I called. Why? Because after I met her in Miami, she quickly became one of my closest, dearest friends, which she still is today. Also, she's a firecracker from the Bronx who I would never, ever want to cross. I knew she would be perfect for the show.

The thing is, Evelyn can sound and act crazy, but when you're her friend she is the kindest, sweetest person in the world. She will give you the shirt off her back, and she'll kill someone if they hurt you. Who wouldn't want a friend like that?

She said yes, and I had my first cast member. Evelyn also had a friend who was married at the time to a player who was retiring. This lady was a very proper New Yorker who grew up with money and was sort of a living Barbie doll. Everything about her was perfect. I loved her, but some people hated her, not just because she was gorgeous but because she tended to look down her nose at people. To me, that meant good television, because nobody watches reality

TV to see someone boring and ordinary. And so, I had my first two wives.

I kept calling NBA wives and girlfriends, and kept adding names to my cast list. I confirmed a Miami Heat cheerleader who was also dating a major NBA star, and two other wives who I knew were interesting and potentially entertaining. I had a great idea, and I had a cast. Now I had a show to pitch.

So . . . how do you pitch a TV show?

As I mentioned, I had worked at *Access Hollywood* for a while and met a few producers, but I had no idea how to sell my show or who to even talk to about it. Eventually, I called a couple of friends in the business and asked them how TV worked. They introduced me to people who worked for production companies, and I was able to set up a few meetings. If I could get a production company on board with my idea, I would be able to then pitch the show to networks as a complete package: the idea, the cast members, and the behind-the-camera production team, already put together.

I showed up at production company offices with the bios of four of the ladies who had agreed to be part of the cast, the details about my idea, and that was it. No sizzle reel or storyboards. Looking back, I was terribly naive to think I could just walk into meetings with what I had and pitch a show, but keep in mind, I was doing all this before reality TV had become a billion-dollar industry. There weren't a lot of rules. I said, "My idea is a reality show called *Basketball Wives*. You're just going to follow us while we do whatever we do. I've got three friends. This one is crazy. This one is a socialite snob. This one is sweet."

Everyone loved it. By this time, the *Real Housewives* franchise was in full swing, with shows based in Orange County, Atlanta, New

Jersey, New York, and Washington, D.C., and that helped the appeal of *Basketball Wives*. Within a few weeks, I had chosen a production company and now we had a package: a show concept, a cast, an executive producer (me), and a company that would handle everything from preproduction to location scouting to wardrobe to filming the actual episodes. Now all we needed was a network. It was one of the most exciting times of my life.

Despite how simple I'd kept my pitch, I had a clear vision of what I wanted the show to be. I was fine with drama. It's necessary in reality TV so that viewers have people to root for and against. Without that, nobody watches. But we would not *manufacture* drama. I didn't want staged catfights. I wanted real life. Despite the public image of NBA wives, I had never witnessed actual basketball wives fighting with each other. I knew some who didn't like each other, but that's normal in any group of people. But physically fighting and throwing drinks and all that? I'd never seen that, and I didn't want a show based on that.

I didn't want the show to be about infidelity either. We would not roll around in the gutter. Evelyn might want to kill any woman her boyfriend was messing with, but we weren't going to talk about that on *Basketball Wives*. We wouldn't trash side pieces or talk about mistresses. We didn't need to create drama anyway; we had Evelyn! I adore her—an opinionated, unstoppable girl who's very raw, very real, and very blunt. Things would come out of her mouth that would make a twenty-year navy veteran blush. Evelyn would give the show its edge.

However, I knew all of us could also sit down at a table and have candid conversations about our lives over lunch, or just go shopping together. We were all very different, but we all got along, and I thought our everyday lives would be fun for people to see. Naturally, there would be some conflict, but there would also be laughter and honesty and women being friends and supporting each other. I wanted to let people peek behind the curtain and see what it was really like to be an NBA wife—good, bad, and otherwise.

Now that I had my initial cast and a production company on board, it was time to pitch the show. When you pitch a show like mine, you're not asking a network to buy the rights (I still own those). Instead, you're asking them to green-light it, which means they agree to pay for production in return for the exclusive rights to broadcast the show. My production company set up pitch meetings with BET, VH1, MTV, and Fox. All of them were extremely interested.

I was still technically married, which to some of the TV executives meant they would get a juicy inside look at my marriage. I let them go ahead and think that, but it was never going to happen. Some of them clearly wanted to turn this into *The Shaunie and Shaquille Show*. Not a chance. When I was pitching the show, I was all but certain I was going to get a divorce, and as it turned out I made a deal with VH1 just a few weeks before I filed. In just thirty days, *Basketball Wives* had gone from an idea to a green-lit show, and I was now an executive producer!

Until my marriage to Keion, Basketball Wives was the most exciting thing ever to happen to me, other than the birth of my kids. I was going to make something that had nothing to do with my marriage, even though I was only a basketball wife because of that marriage. But this was my story to tell. My ex-husband didn't get me in the door. I had done that on my own. I was determined to be financially independent, no matter what happened in the future.

As we went into preproduction for season one, we decided to shoot mostly in Miami, because that's where most of the ladies I had chosen for the cast were based. I was pre-divorce when I pitched the show, which meant I was still in Orlando, and so was one of the other girls, so it just made sense to stay in Florida for the first season. By the time we started production, I had made the big break from my marriage and moved back to Los Angeles, so eventually the show ended up there, too.

Everyone was excited, because reality TV was very lucrative; the ratings were big, and the costs were relatively low. But I was careful. I kept the rights to everything. I already had additional shows in mind. I was in this for the long run.

I also would not compromise on my vision for a show that was honest, real, and non-exploitative, which might sound strange if you know reality television—and especially if you know shows like the *Real Housewives*. The image of women in reality TV is that we're crazy—throwing drinks, pulling hair, cursing each other out, just a bunch of overdressed, shallow, self-absorbed gold diggers. But that is far from the truth of our real lives (at least for most of us).

Unfortunately, from the beginning, certain people have tried to reduce my show to just catfights and bitchiness. Writing about *Basketball Wives LA* for *The Hollywood Reporter*, David Knowles said, "[It] is, first and foremost, a show about fighting and arguing, and its short-tempered, backstabbing cast has been assembled for just that purpose. As with its forerunner, the NBA stars receive scant screen time in this drama; the bulk of the action takes place far away from the Staples

Center. Instead, we follow their significant others as they drift around town—from shoe shopping on Rodeo Drive, to afternoon drinks at Venice Beach's Hotel Erwin, to, yes, the inevitable acting class."

I hate that characterization. Sure, I knew bringing together a bunch of opinionated, hot-blooded NBA wives and girlfriends had the potential to throw off a lot of drama. But the truth about the show is a lot more nuanced than some reporter's snark. What you see on-screen with *Basketball Wives* is not the reality of these women, or of me. Nobody's writing lines for us. We're improvising bigger, brassier versions of ourselves. But away from the set, we're colleagues and friends. The grudges and catfights, unless someone said something really out of line, are forgotten. We go out for coffee or drinks or a late dinner and spend time laughing and talking about our lives, just like you and your friends.

In other words, we're *acting*. Every woman on the show now, and every woman who's ever lasted more than a few episodes in the past, has understood that we're making entertainment, not a documentary. *Our real lives are not that interesting.* If you followed me around on a typical day, I wouldn't be walking the red carpet wearing a couture gown or refereeing a catfight between two women about who'd slept with whose man. I'd be going to Trader Joe's and Target, having Face-Time calls with my kids, making dinner for me and my husband, and going to bed early.

None of the women on the show, even the ones who've become infamous for out-of-control behavior and wild stunts, are like what you see on-screen. Those are characters they've created to keep fans watching because conflict and controversy drive ratings. And if there's anyone who embodies the reality of *Basketball Wives*, it's Evelyn. I can't tell the story of the show without telling her story. She's the cast member I'm closest with in real life. I've known her for at least fifteen years, and she remains one of my best friends.

On the show Evelyn has always been portrayed as crazy and volatile, and fans give me a hard time because they assume I condone her violence and vulgarity, but ninety-nine percent of the time that is not who she is. You can push her to that place, but when the cameras are off, Evelyn is nothing like the woman you see on the show. She's a loving mother, a smart businesswoman, and a fierce friend. She's compassionate, sweet, and smart. For example, Evelyn has done charitable work that never shows up on camera, a lot of it with victims of domestic violence, because she is a domestic violence survivor herself.

Evelyn took that experience and decided she didn't want other women to suffer like she had. In 2017, she ran an online campaign called "Turn Hurt into Joy" that raised money to help survivors escape the violence and start new lives. Then in 2018, she started her own foundation, the Evelyn Lozada Foundation, to empower women and girls through health and wellness, education, and entrepreneurship. That's who Evelyn is: a tough-as-nails survivor with a heart of gold. When she's not on camera, she's with her kids, just like I used to be. She's also a terrific entrepreneur who has her own jewelry and fitness clothing lines, has published two novels, and has used her huge social media following to support Black-owned businesses. She's an amazing lady.

Evelyn will also fight at the slightest provocation, and over the years that's powered some of the most dramatic *Basketball Wives* moments.

She knows she shouldn't let her temper get out of control, but some-times she can't help it. We've talked about it many times. Before each season, she and I have inspirational talks where I'll say, "Listen, you gotta grow up. You gotta not let people push your buttons." She'll look at me and say, "Yes, I know, you're right. I'm gonna change things this year." Then the season starts, and someone pushes her buttons and she goes nuclear. If you've watched the show, you've seen it. You can probably predict it.

She and I are both Sagittarius, but we're so different. If I love and care about you, I might share how I feel about something, and even be brutally honest, but I'm never going to turn the scene into a brawl. That's not me. But when Evelyn is mad, she cannot control her-self. She'll cut so deeply with her words that she draws blood. During the 2019 season, she and this new girl argued for forty-five minutes straight. It was insane, but also kind of impressive—insults, back and forth, nonstop, like two tennis stars at Wimbledon. The rest of the cast and crew stopped what we were doing and just watched in awe. Finally, the other woman just got tired, because she finally threw up her hands and walked away.

Having Evelyn go off on you is a *Basketball Wives* rite of passage. She was at the center of one of the show's classic moments. In season two, one of the newer cast members found out that Evelyn had had a relationship with the man who later became this other woman's husband. It came up on the show, and we played it up for some "You messed with my man" drama, but when the cameras turned off every-one thought it was done.

Later that evening we were all out at a restaurant in South Beach, celebrating the birthday of another cast member, and the "you messed with my man" thing came up again. Before we knew it, these two women were brawling with each other in the street in front of the restaurant—a scratching, hair-pulling, knock-down, drag-out fight. I was in the middle, trying to hold them apart, and production assistants were jumping in and trying to break it up.

Finally, the women calmed down and we all went home, but the next day everyone was covered in bruises and scratches, including me. Evelyn called me and said, "Oh my God, what the hell happened last night?" Production had shut down for the day because the network and producers didn't know what to do after this huge fight. Instead, everyone came to my hotel, and we went to hang out by the pool. Then I got a call from the woman Evelyn had fought with.

"What are you doing?"

"Sitting by the pool."

"Okay, I'm coming over."

This was not good. "I have to stay at this hotel," I said. "I don't want any problems."

"Girl, whatever." *Click.*

She was on her way. Now I was expecting disaster. A few minutes later this woman walked into the pool area, and we all held our breath. Would this start a fight that would kill the show? Instead, she just lay down on a lounge chair, turned her face to the sun, and said, "Hey girls, what y'all doing?" It was like nothing had ever happened. It had all been an act. Evelyn and I looked at each other and thought, *Damn, we have a really good cast member here.*

Over the years Evelyn and all the other incredible women of *Basketball Wives* have produced some unforgettable moments, on-screen and off. There was Evelyn delivering her classic line in the middle of a fight: "You're a non-motherfucking factor!" People still say that to me to this day; Evelyn even had T-shirts made. There was the cast member who laid down an on-camera warning to every new girl who joined the show: "Listen, I don't know you, you don't know me. You keep my name out of your mouth unless you're talking to my face, and then we can figure it out. Other than that, if I hear something behind my back, we're going to have a problem." You would see these poor girls' eyes get wide and terrified.

Jackie Christie was the unofficial mom of our crazy on-screen family. I would describe Jackie this way: If she loves you, she loves you *hard*. No other *Basketball Wives* cast member cares more about how the season is going than Jackie. She wants nothing more than the show's success, and I love and appreciate her for that. Jackie is also quick to remind the other ladies that she is a veteran of the show, a mother, and has a devoted husband who she remarries every year. She's sweet as can be but will get the craziest look in her eyes if you cross her. I don't think she likes it, but I love to describe her as "the best kind of crazy, with a whole lot of love."

When the cameras are off, Jackie is the one checking on everybody, making sure everyone has what they need. She has everybody's phone number and always makes sure everybody is okay. She cares about everything, worries about everyone, and gets angry about any perceived slight or threat. She's also constantly starting businesses—a record label, a TV production company, a publishing company, makeup lines, candles, sex toys, you name it. I think she's up to eighteen and still going.

And yes, Jackie and her husband, Doug, get remarried every year in a real wedding ceremony, which is an incredibly romantic tradition.

One year, we were shooting for two weeks in Portugal, and Doug surprised her by showing up to throw their wedding. But one of the cast members and I had taken the day off from filming, and when we got back we felt terrible. But I had an idea to make it up to them. I asked the production team to get us tons of roses, and we removed each rose petal by hand and covered the roof of their hotel in them, then hired a Portuguese guitar player to serenade them while they had dinner and danced.

Thanks to the passions of some of the ladies on the show, *Basketball Wives* has gotten involved with causes such as helping the homeless. Cast members have passed out gifts to kids in need in Compton or participated in the Book Bank Foundation's annual "Shelter from the Streets" holiday bus tour, riding through New York City's five boroughs, giving needy kids toys and winter clothes. Cast members have started brands and businesses, clothing and jewelry lines, charitable foundations, and nonprofits to help causes they really care about.

The women who have appeared on *Basketball Wives*, past and present, in all its cities, are a lot more than basketball wives. That's a message I'll never stop sending. We're much more than hairdos, nails, and couture. We're mothers, sisters, entrepreneurs, and people who are trying to make a positive difference in the world. We're powerful Black women with our own identities. We're even role models. For all the drama, fights, and craziness, we are women of substance.

Sure, our conversations can be gossipy, and we have drama, but we also do things together, real things. We aren't always shopping, traveling, and having dinner and cocktails. We're raising our kids. We're trying to find love. Some of us are trying to keep marriages alive, while others are just discovering new marriages. We're all incredibly lucky to do what we do, but it's important to acknowledge that it's not easy to put your personal life on display for the public. Something always has to give. One season, my dad was diagnosed with advanced diabetes and spent a month in the hospital. I wouldn't film for a couple of weeks because I was taking my turn to sit with him.

Unfortunately, after a few years I started to see *Basketball Wives* take a turn for the worse. It became trashier, until it seemed like the only thing the network cared about was the content that drove ratings—fights and ugliness. Unfortunately, there was little I could do about it. The ratings drove everything.

By now, some of the ladies were making good money on their own and had been able to become financially independent from the men in their lives, which had been my own goal. Some were even able to quit full-time jobs and become full-time *Basketball Wives* cast members instead.

By season three, our crew of thirty or forty people had also become a family. Some of them even said to me, "Thank you so much for providing such an awesome place for us to be able to earn a living." I was enjoying it too. I was earning my own money and was able to use child support money exclusively for my kids. I wasn't about to walk away from the show and bring an end to all that. But that meant I had to watch my creation turn into something I never dreamed of and didn't want it to be. I felt helpless.

So many times I went to the network to say, "You know, this is not what I envisioned. Can we reel it in and leave in some of the good, positive stuff we're filming?" During one season—season three or four—they allowed us to pull back on a fight because I made a big stink about it. Immediately, when the ratings went down (they had been low all season) network executives blamed it on that decision: "Hey, we tried what you wanted. It just doesn't work. That's not what your fans want. You want to be renewed? You want another season? Then we need more of Evelyn and the other women at each other's throats." We went right back to trash.

I have the power to edit myself. I don't have the power to edit anybody else. I always keep my family in mind when thinking about how all the drama will play out. I'm never going to go on camera and act like a total jackass, because I don't want to embarrass my kids. I don't want to embarrass my mother. We all make mistakes, but I'll be damned if I'm going to be on national TV fighting with another grown woman, throwing a wine bottle, or doing anything that reflects badly on my family or my husband. I even put a lot of thought into how I dress on TV, because it all impacts the overall impression I make on people.

I may be the only person in reality TV who thinks this way. If I'm doing a show and it's spiraling out of control, the only thing I can do is conduct myself in a manner that reflects who I really am and remain true to myself. But for several seasons, the show became about women arguing all the time, and even if I conducted myself with class, I got backlash. Eventually, things became so embarrassing that I thought about walking away from *Basketball Wives*.

The trouble was, I didn't know how to leave the show without destroying it. I am the show's creator and its most visible personality. If I had said, "I don't want to be a part of this anymore," I was quite sure that would have brought the whole franchise down, which would have left the cast and crew unemployed. Some of the ladies had started businesses and would be fine, but the crew was able to pay their mortgages because of *Basketball Wives*. They depended on me. So, I struck a kind of devil's bargain. I didn't say anything, but I figured maybe I could become so boring that the producers would sort of wean me from the storyline. Maybe I would show up one day on set in sweats and rollers with no makeup on, and the producers would take me aside and say, "Hey, Shaunie, we don't really *need* you on camera anymore. How about you take your executive producer check and just be behind the scenes, okay?"

I kept a low profile like that for two or three seasons. If you watched those seasons and noticed that I had become the person tagging along without much of an opinion on anything, now you know why. But it didn't work. I was stuck. I came to a meeting to talk about the next season and the producers pitched me some sleazy storyline about one of the girls confronting another girl about her having an affair with my ex-husband while we were married. It wasn't true. But that didn't matter. They accused her on camera, which pulled me in because I was expected to be outraged. "Did you know about this? Have you heard this? Who do you believe?" We had a whole season of this, and it was great TV, but I hated it.

As it turned out, so did a lot of other people. My experience at the Essence Music Festival made that painfully clear. In 1995, *Essence* magazine marked its twenty-fifth anniversary, and to celebrate, the publishers threw what was supposed to be a onetime festival. Today, that onetime event has become "the party with a purpose"—the country's biggest, most important celebration of African American culture and music, taking over the streets of New Orleans every July. Being asked to participate was a big deal for me.

In July 2011, after *Basketball Wives* had wrapped its second hit season, Evelyn and I, along with some other cast members, appeared at the Louisiana Superdome for the Essence Music Festival along with NeNe Leakes of *Real Housewives of Atlanta*. The scene was pandemonium: crowds of cheering, screaming ladies giving us their enthusiasm, love, and pride for what we had created, something that brought Black women's stories to millions. I was grateful but stunned. I'd experienced fan adoration before while with Shaquille, but this was different. This time, the love was for me and what I had made, and it was a validation of everything I had worked and sacrificed for—my independence, my vision, my self-determination, and my role as a leader among Black women. It was an incredible day.

Just a few years later, that triumph had turned angry and bitter. The show had become more sensationalistic. Explorations of female friendships and Black women's issues? *Gone*. The show became mostly about bottle-throwing catfights, screaming matches, and manufactured drama. Ratings soared, but the community of Black women that had praised me for telling our true stories turned on me, accusing me of making Black women look angry and crazy. The website Black and Married with Kids called the show "a disgrace to Black women and wives everywhere."

The criticism was savage and painful, but honestly, I had it coming. I had created *Basketball Wives* to uplift Black women, but it had morphed into something tawdry, and I had failed to right the ship. As we became more vulgar and the on-screen scandals heated up, fans let me have it on social media. I was a hypocrite. I was a sellout. I had betrayed them. I should be fired as executive producer. Ratings nosedived.

I deserved at least some of the criticism. I had been in a position to counter harmful stereotypes, and I had perpetuated them because I liked having a top-rated show. It was easy for angry fans to convince the world that I was a manipulator exploiting people for ratings.

In 2021, things got so bad that I did a test screening to be one of the new hosts for *The Real*. I prayed they would choose me, because it would have given me a legitimate reason to leave *Basketball Wives* while giving them a chance to keep the franchise going without me. I didn't end up being selected, but after a few more years of *Basketball Wives* going in what I considered the wrong direction, things are finally looking better. With BET on board, I'm confident we'll be able to keep the show authentic and entertaining while dealing with some more serious issues and steering away from wild-eyed fights that reinforce the stereotype that Black women are crazy and dangerous.

I wish I could figure out how to get as many fans to watch a show about complex, big-hearted, smart women being partners, mothers, and businesswomen as are willing to watch a show about women screaming insults and throwing shoes. I'd like to show women figuring out how to move on after a divorce, like I did. I'd like to show what it's like to go into business meetings and have your ideas rejected because, even now, you're the only Black woman in the room.

In the meantime, I will do my best to keep *Basketball Wives* as real and honest as possible. It's the longest-running reality show ever created by a Black woman, and I'm incredibly proud of that. When I finally find the right formula to make it the show I think it can be, I'll let you know.

CHAPTER 7

JUGGLING ACT

For more than ten years, I was in a relationship where money was not an issue, which meant I was able to be a full-time mom without having to worry about working. Believe me, I know how lucky I was to have that time and security. It gave me the freedom to focus on my children in a way that many other mothers can't. True, a lot of mothers have jobs or other commitments that make giving time to Girl Scouts or school fundraisers more difficult, but they find a way. I get that. I've also seen moms in Hollywood who have wealthy spouses and all the time in the world and still choose to hand their kids off to a nanny so they can go shopping at Hermès and Prada.

I always saw being a mother as my first job, even when it was just me and Myles and my nine-to-five. In the mornings when I got him up, I made sure that as I was getting dressed for work I engaged him in conversation. I didn't want to just sit him in front of the TV. I'd go back and forth while putting my makeup on, making sure he was eating his breakfast. I might set my breakfast down on the table next to him, even if that meant me taking a bite, going back to continue getting dressed, and then returning to the table.

On the car ride to preschool, we would put in a CD. It might be Barney, it might be *Blue's Clues* songs, whatever Myles liked at the time. We sang the songs together all the way to school. When I worked at Fox, I had an hour-and-a-half lunch, so sometimes I would drive to the school and have lunch with him. I wanted to be with him as much as possible whenever I wasn't working.

Even with my kids now, even though most of them are grown, being their mom is still my number one priority. Shareef might have a team banquet in April and I'm texting him, asking, "When is it? Can I be there?" He would love that, but he's not going to ask me. He's a young adult man, and young adult men don't ask their mothers to come to events, even if they want them to. So, I have to engage.

I think my determination to be present for as much of my children's lives as possible came from the pain I felt because my dad, the most important man in my life, wasn't present for mine. My mom came to see the things I did when I was growing up, but my dad not so much. I never understood why.

Later, when I was older, I asked him about it. "Daddy, how come you never came to my recitals or plays?" He told me he always felt like he didn't fit in with the parents who did that kind of stuff. He didn't feel like he could talk to them. "I just didn't feel comfortable," he said. "I didn't have those kinds of clothes, and I didn't want them looking at me like I was crazy."

My dad was a "street" kind of guy. When he was growing up, he mostly hung out in pool halls and places like that, and his friends were mostly street thugs. He felt like he didn't fit the upper-echelon lifestyle he wanted us to have. He wanted me to be in the arts and do sophisticated things, but he didn't feel like he belonged. So, he hung back, not realizing that I was always looking for him and how much it would have meant to me if he had shown up.

I've talked with Keion about this because he's divorced and coparenting and only gets to see his daughter every other weekend. He has a lot of guilt over missing any of her events. He's such a good man, and he wants to be a spectacular dad, and he *is* a spectacular dad, but he overcompensates. He finds himself buying his daughter things or sending her things to compensate for having to miss events. If he hears she's having pajama day at school, he'll tell me how he's going to buy her some pajamas and a blanket and send them to the house. That's so sweet, because he's so sincere, but I always remind him, "I bet she won't remember that pajama and blanket, but I'll bet she never forgets you showing up for things."

My kids have gotten some extravagant gifts from their father, who can buy them anything. Once, when they were small, he offered to buy each of them their own custom-made golf cart. Since when does a child in elementary school need a golf cart? I was usually the bad guy, so I put my foot down and we ended up compromising: the kids got a couple of custom golf carts they could share. Ridiculous, I know. Since *Basketball Wives* became a hit, I've been able to give them plenty of material comforts, too. But they never talk about that stuff. Possessions don't make memories. Instead, the kids say things like, "Remember the time I won that game, and you were there and that was so amazing?" That's why I work so hard to be present.

.   .   .

When I became a single parent after my divorce, my devotion to my kids didn't change. I still made sure to show up for as many games, plays, and dances as I could. I might be there for one kid and miss something for the others, but over a typical month it would all balance out. My kids knew I was there. I calendared everything, wrote down everything, and used every second of the day. If I could take an important call on the way to a basketball game, I did. Those fifteen minutes in the car would free me to watch my daughter play without distractions.

Once I started *Basketball Wives* the juggling act became more challenging. The kids were all small, ranging from elementary to middle school, and while we lived in Los Angeles, we began shooting the first season in Miami. How could I possibly manage to be in Florida executive producing my show and appearing as a cast member and still be an attentive mother? The answer was obvious: *I would bring the kids with me!* It was summer and there was no school, so it was (relatively) easy to get the six of us on a flight to Miami and live in a hotel for a while. The kids saw it as a big adventure.

Still, it impacted the show. If you go back to season one, I wasn't on the show very often because I would not compromise on not leaving my kids. With all that was happening with our family, they needed their mom. I even told the producers I was okay with walking away if they couldn't accommodate me, because at that time I needed to be there for my children. It was my way or the highway, and there was no room for compromise. From time to time I got pushback, until they figured out it would be a lot easier for everybody if they just included my kids in the show.

Some people had a tough time wrapping their heads around that idea. This wasn't a family show. It was about the ladies and their drama. But I forced the producers' hands. They came to understand, *If we want Shaunie to participate, we're going to have to adapt to her. She doesn't compromise about her kids.* I am the only cast member who had her kids as a part of her on-screen life from beginning to end. In season two, we did a scene at Shaquille's house in Orlando. He wasn't there, but the kids were because he had them for a week for spring break and I went to pick them up. The crew wanted to film that because it was real. The kids had no problem with any of it. Because of their dad, they've been around cameras their entire lives. It's what they knew.

With my kids around, days on the set during that first season required a lot of adapting. I would have my hair and makeup done in my hotel room because I couldn't leave. I would plan my day on the set while simultaneously planning activities for the kids. Sometimes, my cousin or our wonderful housekeeper, Veronica (who became sort of a nanny and is still part of our family today), would travel with me and help out. This is a typical example of one of our conversations: "I shoot from noon to four o'clock. How about I take them to the pool for an hour, then I'll come back, change clothes, regroup, eat dinner with them, then go back and shoot again. Oh, and can you take Myles to a movie?" It was as chaotic as it sounds, but I desperately wanted this new career to succeed, and I would do anything to make it all work.

When the new school year rolled around, my strategy had to change. Now I would only shoot on weekends, but that still meant I was flying from L.A. to Miami on Friday afternoons and flying back on Sunday nights. When I was on set, the crew worked me hard because that was all the time they had with me. As soon as my plane touched down in Florida, I was in hair and makeup. Sixteen-hour days on the set were common for me.

After those long weekends, I would be totally exhausted, but on Monday I would drop the kids off at school and it was right back into mom mode, still determined not to miss things. Thank goodness we only had one more season of shooting in Miami before moving the show to L.A., because I'm not sure how much longer I could have kept up with that schedule and those hours.

Back then, if you had asked me what I did for self-care, I would have shrugged and told you "Not much." Self-care has never been on my radar, even when I had a houseful of little ones and could have really used it! When it was just me and Myles, my self-care time was in the evening after feeding him and putting him to bed. I might take a moment to watch TV before going to sleep and getting up for work the next day. When I was married and had multiple kids, I learned to nap when they did, and when they went to school, I didn't have anything else going on.

I did try to figure out ways to do things I thought I might enjoy. I took yoga classes and went for walks. At one point when we lived in Phoenix, I bought an ATV and during the day, when it wasn't too hot, I would ride it around the mountains. I can be a real tomboy, and I love riding ATVs. To this day, I love going somewhere I can drive dune buggies or ATVs. That's still self-care for me, even if I don't call it that. I suppose my real self-care is being busy doing things I love with people I respect.

I wish I could say the production team and the network were behind me one hundred percent from the beginning, but that's not true. Early on I thought it was going to be a problem, because when the show first started, I had two showrunners, both men, neither of whom were parents, and so they were annoyed with me all the time. They dreaded even asking me to do things because they assumed there would be complications related to my kids. Sometimes they were sarcastic: "I guess Myles has another game, right?" They just didn't get it. But as time went on, they came around and understood what I was doing.

Eventually, the team and the network came to respect my wishes and made things work when I was in town because they knew how much I loved my children and was committed to being a good mom. They were truly wonderful, and they made a stressful time much easier.

Not long ago a mom I hadn't been in contact with since Shareef was in high school reached out to me on Instagram. We ended up having a call to catch up, and she asked me about Amirah playing basketball. She said, "Are you still showing up to games with a full face of makeup and in wardrobe?"

That took me back. Sometimes when *Basketball Wives* was shooting, I would come straight from the set to one of my children's games in full TV makeup, wearing whatever outfit I'd been wearing to film, because I didn't have a chance to change. If people didn't know what was going on in my life, they were probably leaning over to each other and muttering, "Who's the drag queen?" It was that level of makeup.

Back in the day, there were times I would leave a shoot right in the middle of a really good scene. I'd say, "I'm sorry, but my son has a game in thirty minutes," and be out the door. The crew would hold certain scenes and film others when I got back. Other times, they would have a scene that had escalated to a climax, and they would have to figure out how to fit me in because I was the nucleus of the episode. My obsession with attending my kids' activities caused a lot of maneuvering on productions, and I'm sure the crew and producers were frustrated with me several times. But my kids were going to come first, no matter what.

We all had to be flexible. More than once as we were leaving a basketball game I had to say, "Guys, just give me an hour. I have to go shoot this, and I'll feed you while you're on the set. Just give me some patience, please." They were good sports about it. I would bring the whole bunch with me, and they would sit off to the side for an hour, perfectly quiet. It was just part of life. I don't know if it ever was fun for them, though. It was just "mom's work."

After a while, they got to know the cast and crew and everybody became like family. The crew would let them play with the equipment, that sort of thing. Plus, they got to know what was going to be on the show before anyone else. For instance, one of the ladies might be acting crazy, and they would get to see it firsthand. But these were still kids. If the shoot went too long, they got restless and started asking, "Mom, when is it time to go?" or "Can I get somebody to come pick me up?"

Keep in mind that all this coming and going—from shoot to games and back again—was happening in L.A. traffic. The kids played games at locations all over the city, so I didn't always know where I would be coming from or how long it would take me to get there, which meant the crew didn't know when to expect me. Usually, we made it work, though there were times when it didn't. There were definitely things I missed. The network loved all-cast scenes, whether it was a party, the launch of a business, or someone's birthday. Those scenes were always one of the highlights of a season, and I missed several of them due to kids' functions or being stuck on the 405.

The ladies were fantastic about my comings and goings. If they had a problem with me, I never heard a word about it. If you talked to any of them now, they would say, "Shaunie didn't play when it came to her kids." Some of the cast had kids around the ages of my kids, too. Jackie Christie had children, but her husband, Doug, was there when she couldn't be. Even though Evelyn's daughter was an adult, Evelyn understood what my priorities were. Most of the women understood and supported me completely.

Still, once in a while things got out of control. One of the most memorable examples happened several years ago, after one of Shareef's basketball games. I had the day off, and I had taken not only my kids to the game but a couple of my nephews, plus one of my girlfriends and her kids. There were so many of us that I had to rent a Sprinter van to hold us all. We were at the game when I got a call from the production team. Tempers had gotten hot during the scene they were trying to film, and the whole thing had spun out of control. The crew relied on me as the calm person with a level head and asked if I could come and help work out the issue and get things back on track.

I told them this was a nonworking day for me, so they would have to wait until the game was over. When it ended, I went to the location in Culver City where they were shooting. I had no makeup on, and I showed up in whatever I was wearing, probably jeans and a sweatshirt. The cameras met me at the door of the Sprinter to show the viewers how urgently I was needed.

Well, the scene we happened to walk into was one of the ladies throwing a dominatrix-themed bondage party! Outside were all kinds of people dressed for this event, including a man in chaps with his butt hanging out. But I didn't know that the people were there for *Basketball Wives.* Instead, I was thinking, *What is going on in this city?* Meanwhile, my kids were in the van seeing all this and just cracking up. Finally, one of the producers came over, thanked me, told me to ignore the strangely dressed people and follow him inside.

"I just need you to go in there and calm people down," he said as we were talking. The crew was putting a mic on me, and I didn't have time to ask any questions. Finally, I went inside and . . . oh my Lord. There were scorpions in little cages. There were ladies walking around with pasties on their nipples and nothing else. There was a cake shaped like a woman's open legs, complete with a vagina. I don't think the crew was able to use any of the footage of me, because I was in shock and I'm sure my face showed it. I couldn't even talk.

Everybody was obviously having a great time, but the producers knew I would never have come unless there was a problem. I didn't care. It was so vulgar, the doors were locked, and I wanted out. It was awful, but everybody else got a good laugh out of it, I guess.

But juggling being a parent and running a hit reality show isn't all funny stories and practical jokes. It's caused me to have to lose time with my kids, too. When *Basketball Wives* became a hit, we started going abroad to film. Active cast members would be required to travel to locations such as Costa Rica or Amsterdam for ten days at a time. Luckily for me, my mother and sister were on top of things at home, so I knew things weren't going to fall apart while I was gone, but I was still going against what I had told my children—that time with them was the most important thing to me.

Like most parents, I also had to make sacrifices for my kids. About eight years ago I was offered a hosting gig on a daytime talk show. It was going to be a panel show like *The Real*, with women talking about the issues of the day. I would have loved to have done it, but I wasn't willing to uproot the kids again, especially to New York, where we knew nobody. It would have been just too far from home. So I said, "No, thank you." My attitude was that if it was meant to be, it would be, and if it was too hard and disrupted too many things for my family, then it wasn't meant to be.

Of course, just three years ago I had a chance to be on *The Real* for real, with my kids all but grown and out of the house, but it didn't work out. Maybe one of these days I will get a talk show of my own. I'll certainly have a lot to say.

CHAPTER 8

GIRLFRIENDS

As much as I would like for it to be otherwise, in the entertainment industry it's hard to find women who genuinely support you and have your back. It seems like those who are preaching women's empowerment are oftentimes the same women who plot against their fellow women. As I've gotten older, I've learned to make my circle smaller. I consider myself to be a pretty friendly person and I like to be in social environments, but I'm the first to admit I'm very closed off to trusting anyone who's not a good girlfriend.

I have a good group of women around me now who make up my inner circle and have each other's backs. Some are retired and comfortably living life. Some are hardworking nine-to-five ladies. We don't necessarily need anything from each other, where we're constantly asking for favors—it's more about support and love. Okay, truth be told, there's some venting, but also lots of understanding, showing up

. . . it's all those things. And I think at my age—at any age, really—that's all you need.

All but one of my eight closest girlfriends have nothing to do with television or *Basketball Wives*. These are typically women I've known for years, because my friendships tend to endure for quite a long time. I think the shortest amount of time I've known any of my close girlfriends is ten years, but most of them go back fifteen or twenty years, and one of them has been a friend for close to forty years.

The eight of us don't necessarily talk every day, but my kids call all of them "Auntie," and they consider my kids to be their nieces and nephews. Any of us could step in at a moment's notice if needed to take one of the other's kids to the doctor. We're just there for each other.

Any conversation about my closest girlfriends has to start with my oldest friend, Alicia. We've known each other since we were teenagers, and she is the godmother to my children. She was there when every one of them was born. She knows secrets about me no one else will ever know. We share some lifelong memories that can get us laughing and/or crying in seconds, and she and I literally finish each other's sentences.

Monique Payton is another one of my closest girlfriends. Earlier, I mentioned that her kids all call me "Auntie." Well, in 2023 I went to a Warriors-Rockets game because her son, Gary Payton II, plays for the Warriors. As far as I'm concerned, he's my nephew. He's over thirty years old now, but I've known him since he was fourteen. When he heard I was coming to the game, he texted me, "Auntie, I'm not playing. I'm still injured, so you don't have to come." I replied, "Absolutely not. I'll be there. I'm coming to see you." I'm not even a Warriors fan. But those are the kinds of friendships I have.

My inner circle of girlfriends wouldn't be complete without my friend Kim, who has a daughter who comes and stays with us for weeks at a time just to visit. That's just what we do. We're family. We share everything. We stay at each other's houses. We confide in each other. We've been through everything together.

I do have one close girlfriend from *Basketball Wives*, and that's Evelyn Lozada. We talk almost every day. Other friendships on the show have come in waves. Part of that is because I'm not just a cast member, I'm also the show's creator and executive producer. If you're a cast member and you feel like we're friends, we're still not on a level playing field because I'm also your boss. We still have a show to do. I can't always take you aside and tell you, "Hey, in a scene today, somebody is going to say some awful things about you, so be prepared." Because then we're not doing reality TV anymore—we're doing scripted television—and that gives you an inside track over someone else on the show.

There are things girlfriends can say to each other that I can't necessarily say to one of the other cast members, even if I'm supposed to as a friend. I think one of the reasons Evelyn and I are so close is that she understood that part of the business from the beginning. She saw that there were times when I needed to be the executive producer of *Basketball Wives* first, not her friend first, even if that meant I didn't get to warn her about things all the time. She didn't take it personally.

There are women on *Basketball Wives* who hate me for this, or at least don't consider us friends. I don't know if I did anything to cause that, but I do understand that it can be hard to find a safe space between friendship and professional life. We make reality television. That's nothing like a sitcom, where we have lines to deliver. This is supposed to be real life. Still, women have come and gone who I wish I was still friends with, but we just couldn't be because of the business. They couldn't handle me wearing both hats.

It takes a special person to deal with this. That's why I'm thankful that after so many years Evelyn is still here, still trusts me, and still knows I have her best interests at heart. She knows I would never try to hurt her, and she knows that despite the craziness that happens on the show sometimes, it's not my fault. There are other women on the show who get that this is a business, and I love and appreciate them when the cameras aren't on me.

The thing is, I really want these ladies to win. It's not always easy for them to switch from the "on camera" to the "off camera" version of themselves. It's easy for me, but I was never really invested in creating an on-camera version of myself. I'm just Shaunie. I'm the same person on camera as I am off. Television Shaunie is not some made-up persona or strategically crafted brand. It's just me.

Because of this, late in the show I started trying to *avoid* befriending the cast in real life. That might sound strange, but it was much easier to deal with them just as on-camera personalities instead of friends. If we're friends, I'm supposed to go above and beyond to look out for you in ways that I can't be responsible for at the end of the day. I can't be a boss anymore. You won't even respect me once we're friends.

These days, I mostly stay out of the way unless a scene comes up where I have to be on camera. That's made some people conclude that I'm a stuck-up bitch who thinks I'm better than they are because I'm a big executive producer. No, that's just me establishing healthy professional boundaries due to painful experiences I've had to endure along the way.

Still, as much as I love them, I don't know that I've ever really shared my entire story with my girlfriends—at least, not in real time. We were all going through things at the same time. Marriages were failing. Children were being born. Parents were dying. Life became so congested with stuff that I'm sure there were times they thought they couldn't vent to me because I was venting to them—and vice versa. So, I may not have shared my whole story, because I was busy listening to theirs. Even so, we have been there for each other for so long that they've been through everything, from Shareef's open-heart surgery when he was just shy of nineteen to my divorce. These are my girls for life.

One thing they'll tell you about me: It's not easy to win my trust. After all I've been through, I don't know that I would be able to start fresh with a new friend at this point in my life—certainly, not at the same trust level I have with my longtime girlfriends. I've seen too much and experienced too much. I don't know that I care or have the capacity to establish the type of friendship I've got with these women.

That doesn't make me unable to have new friends, because I make new friends all the time. But it's not the same. Those friendships are more surface, more superficial. I'm able to hold them at arm's length. We might go to lunch and hang out but I'm not sharing secrets with you. I'm not sharing details about my personal life. Those friends won't ever come close to occupying the same space as the girlfriends I've had for twenty years.

Plus, investing in new friendships takes a lot of time and effort. With my longtime girlfriends, things are effortless. We finish each other's sentences. We each know what the other needs in the moment without anyone saying a word. It's easy to be around them. There's no drama; in fact, they're a buffer against drama.

My girlfriends are closer to me than almost anyone else. They know everything about me, including the embarrassing things, and they love me anyway. They are my safe space and my comfort. They don't judge and have never steered me wrong. They've never betrayed me. I've got my team and honestly, I don't need anyone else.

We are like the fun bunch. We all live in different states now, so it's harder to get together, but when we are in the same place, watch out. We're going to dinner, we're going to brunch, we're sitting by the pool, we're going out for drinks. We are always going somewhere, and if there's one thing about us, it's that we love to dance—hitting up live music venues where we can sing and get up and dance if we want to.

We love to travel together, get together, talk about life, and laugh. The only thing that saddens me is that right now that doesn't happen often enough. We all used to live in Los Angeles, so it was easy to get together every Sunday. We would barbecue and sit around all day, play games, and let the kids have a good time. Now that we're all in different places, we can't be as spontaneous. We have to plan strategically, and we still don't get to spend as much time together as we'd like.

I think my friends value me because I'm a good listener. If you have a problem, you might not necessarily need me to have a solution. You just need someone to listen and understand your thought process. Understand why you're feeling the way you feel. That's me. I'll take it all in, and then I'm the one who will say, "Okay, what do you think?"

I'm going to do my best to understand where you're coming from without judgment. I'll ask, "Are you telling me this because you want my opinion or my advice, or did you just need me to listen?" I'll be whichever one you need me to be. I pride myself on being what you need in the moment. If I have the resources, I'll be your fixer, too. I will do whatever I can to help you make things better.

It's also possible to lose my friendship. The fastest way to do this is to betray me. Lie to me. Break my trust. Be dishonest. I'll talk about this in the next chapter, but throughout my life—especially when I was an NBA wife—I've had people get close because they wanted to learn things about my family or benefit in some way. Revealing private things about me that I don't want revealed is the worst thing you can do to me.

If you're part of my friendship circle, there are boundaries. If we experience things together, hear things together, see things together, or if I shared private things with you, those stay in that safe, private space. They're not for you to share with anyone outside of that space. If you betray that, we're done. You won't get a second chance. Broken trust cannot be unbroken.

But even if you were to break my trust, I'm not the kind of ex-friend who will talk badly about you or refuse to talk to you the next time I see you. If someone asks me, "Hey, what happened to so-and-so? I thought you guys used to hang out," I'll just answer, "Yeah, not so much anymore." I won't share what happened because I'm not interested in spreading negativity. In fact, I'm more likely to tell the other person all the wonderful things about you. "She was super sweet and my God, she was such a great cook!" I'll compliment you and move on. If I see you, I'll give you a hug. But we will not break bread. We won't sit at a table sharing moments ever again.

Girlfriends are "found family," the family you choose. And you know how seriously I take family.

CHAPTER 9

LIFE IN MY
"PRIVACY BUBBLE"

My life has been quite different from that of the typical wife and mom. I know that, and there's so much about that life for which I will always be grateful. But there are also some differences I still have trouble seeing as blessings. One of them has to do with privacy.

When I got married, I knew I was accepting membership into an exclusive club, that of the NBA wife. I knew membership came with privileges, but one of the most difficult adjustments I had to make was that, like it or not, I was now a semi-celebrity. Now, while nobody would be asking me to autograph a jersey with "Shaunie" on the back, I would still be an occasional target of that popular American pastime: assuming you know what someone is really like just because you know their name and recognize their face. And then when I started a reality show where I and other women put our private lives on display for millions of people, I gave up even more privacy.

You don't even have to be a semi-celebrity to have experienced this. Have you ever posted an opinion on social media and had people you've never met drag you for it? Multiply that by one hundred if you're publicly known. I've told you about when the internet called me a colorist, and when everyone decided, without a shred of proof, that I was getting a divorce because I had committed adultery with my nonexistent personal trainer and had been embezzling from my ex-husband. That's the kind of invasion of privacy that makes you want to seal yourself inside a bubble, and that's exactly what I've done.

Everyone who knows me knows I am an incredibly private person. I guard my private life because I believe that if you don't look at the world with at least a little bit of suspicion, you're not living in reality. Not all people have good intentions. Some have hidden agendas. Some don't want to see you shine because they're afraid you'll make them look bad. Some don't want to see you happy because they're unhappy and misery loves company. You simply can't trust everyone. And while I don't necessarily want to live in a bubble, for the sake of my security and peace of mind, I do.

My bubble is a state of mind. It's an attitude that says when it comes to my personal life and my family, people are untrustworthy until proven otherwise. It's the antidote to the social media impulse that says we should always be sharing our locations, posting endless vacation selfies, and going public with the most intimate details of our lives. I'm active on Instagram, Twitter, and Facebook, but I'm very selective about what I post, and I never post anything in real time.

One reason I'm so careful is that, as much as it bothers me to admit it, women are more vulnerable than men when it comes to being a target. I'm not just talking about physical risk, either. We're judged more harshly than men, and we're more likely to be sexualized or shamed. I'm especially vigilant as the mother of two daughters. A few years ago, one of my daughters befriended a boy on social media. There's nothing wrong with that, but things quickly got to a place that I felt was inappropriate. He was asking her for pictures (she was underage), and she was flattered, sending him emojis and the like. I understand. It feels good to have a boy like you. But I had no idea who this guy was, and I shut it down.

I can do things like that because I practice what I preach. I don't do dumb things like texting Keion suggestive pictures. Today, that's an incredibly reckless thing for any woman to do, especially someone in the public eye like I am. Our private life is *private*, and I get great peace of mind from knowing that if somebody ever says they have compromising pictures of me, they're lying. Those pictures do not exist.

Does my way seem lonely, or even paranoid? It might look like that. But what's truly unhealthy is how social media has distorted our concept of friendship. When I was growing up in middle-class Los Angeles, my friends were peers who I got to know at school or church. We played together, met each other's families, had sleepovers, and shared time at barbecues and summer camps. We trusted each other because we'd known each other for years. We had history, shared interests, and community.

Now, a "friend" is anyone who follows you on social media. They ask you for entry into your personal life, and you say, "Sure, come on in." It's crazy because *you do not know these people*. You might feel like you do, but you really don't. There's nothing to stop people on social media from turning on you, and some do. I've been there.

Years ago, some thieves tried to rob our house while we were at Disneyland. They knew we were at Disneyland because the kids were posting in real time that we were there and what we were doing. I knew nothing about it because I wasn't on my phone. We had one of those Ring doorbells with a camera, and it kept going off, but we also had a dog that kept setting off our Ring, so I had mostly stopped looking at the alerts. I just happened to look at my phone one day, and I saw these guys trying to scale our wall. I yelled out, and they heard me through the Ring's speaker, and it scared them away. They thought we were inside the house.

Back when he was twelve, one of my sons had someone steal his identity on social media. It turned out to be a grown man in Pittsburgh who was into child pornography, and he was using my boy's name, pictures, avatar, everything. A police officer came to our house and asked us all kinds of questions, which was unnerving because we hadn't gotten any weird calls or direct messages. The police ended up tracking the creep down, but it was scary.

It's not just social media, either. Misunderstandings between *Basketball Wives* cast members have been blown up into viral scandals. Every aspect of my separation and divorce was gossiped about, misrepresented, or turned into a personal attack. I was attacked for posting a family Christmas photo on Instagram in 2020 because we weren't wearing masks . . . in our own home. When Keion and I are out in public or sitting on a plane, I've watched people sneak their phones out and film us, thinking I won't notice. The old Shaunie wouldn't have said anything, but now I confront them. "I see what you're doing," I'll say. "Would you please respect our privacy?" They blush and then stammer, "What? Oh, no. I wasn't filming you."

Look, I get it. You want to catch a celebrity in the wild. But I would rather you just ask me for a picture, because then I don't feel stalked. The fact is, while I might choose to politely say no, if you ask nicely I'm probably going to agree to a picture 99.9 percent of the time. I would rather you just not take my picture when I'm shoving a bunch of french fries in my mouth.

Some of my insistence on a privacy bubble comes from my experiences as an NBA girlfriend and wife. During those ten years, I met a lot of very nice people who wanted access to our lives and said, "They're like family, it's all good." Then they turned around and burned us by talking too much about things that should have remained private. More than once, we were traveling in a foreign country with friends and having a great time only to see details and pictures of our vacation on social media or on the local news. We shouldn't have to police our friends to make sure they don't stab us in the back.

Finally, the rumors, lies, and attacks became too much, and I decided to build my privacy bubble. Now I choose who I allow into my life and the lives of my family members . . . and believe me, my standards are high.

Not everyone understands how fiercely I safeguard my private life. Some people are put off by it. When I started dating Keion, I explained my bubble to him, and his response was, "That's no way to live." I get that. His approach is to love and welcome everybody, and then when they burn you, let them go. I love that he's that way, but I can't live like that. My approach is more like, "I'm going to keep you at arm's length until you earn enough of my trust that I feel comfortable allowing you into a space where you could burn me. Even then, I'm probably never letting you in all the way."

I wish I could be more like Keion, but I can't. His life experience is different from mine. Yes, he leads a large congregation and needs to conduct himself with discretion, but he hasn't been exposed and attacked like I have. I've made small talk with a woman who I knew was having an affair with the husband of one of my good friends . . . and said nothing to either woman. I didn't tell my friend because I knew she would never leave her husband, so why cause her the kind of pain I had experienced? I've vacationed with couples where I knew one or both partners were cheating and said nothing. It matters to me that you can trust me, even if I can't trust you.

From my first date with Keion, my insistence on keeping people at arm's length was an issue. He noticed that I wouldn't let our relationship move any faster than walking speed, even though I really liked him from the beginning. But on that first night, I was incredibly careful not to reveal anything too intimate, and I could tell he knew I was slow-playing things. I'm fine with that. My guarded nature can annoy some people, and that's all right. If you resent the fact that I'm not an open book after one date, you don't belong in my circle.

Finally, after a few more dates, Keion spoke up. "I've noticed that I'll share my things with you, and you only share half your things with me," he said. I told him that's just who I am, and to his credit, he accepted that, though he obviously didn't understand it. But if he had disrespected my desire to safeguard my privacy and personal life, would I have walked away from this wonderful man, who has become the love of my life?

No, of course not. I know a good thing when I see it. I would have likely opened up a dialogue with him to help him really understand my life experience and why I felt such an urgent need to safeguard my privacy. Because he's a compassionate and empathetic man, I'm sure he would have come to accept my need for discretion and caution, as he has.

After Keion learned about my bubble, we talked about it extensively. He didn't judge me for it; he just wanted to learn why it was so important to me. Gradually, as I got to know him, because he is such a good man, and because I fell madly in love with him, I lowered my defenses. He eventually came to accept that I'm not sharing my business with anybody I don't trust completely, and if he wanted to be a part of my life, he would have to respect that. Fortunately for me, he does.

I'm extremely good at discerning people's intentions, their level of genuineness, and the discretion with which they communicate. That's what makes my bubble possible. After a couple of interactions with a new person, I can peg whether or not I can trust them with my privacy. Once someone has given me the sense that they're going to be careless with my privacy, they fall outside the "bubble" category. People who fall outside might include the person who always has to know everybody else's business, the one who's not careful about the conversations they have in crowded public places, or the friend who overshares on social media.

If you're always butt-dialing someone or accidentally texting someone something they weren't supposed to see, you're too much of a risk for me. Those breaches, even if they're accidental, are a violation of my privacy bubble. I can't risk that kind of carelessness in my world. That doesn't mean I don't like you, and it doesn't mean we aren't friends. You just won't ever set foot inside my bubble.

My other main rule for my bubble is clear and simple. If someone doesn't need to know what I'm doing, they don't get to know. Since my father died in 2022, I talk to my mother every day, but I don't call her and my siblings and share everything that's going on with me, because they don't need to know that. If I go out of town, I'll let my mom know so she doesn't worry, and of course Keion and my kids know where I am. But that's it. Nobody else, not even my sister, Cori, has "know what Shaunie is up to" privileges. Like most siblings, my sister, brother, and I don't keep tabs on each other all the time.

Keion is the opposite. He's gregarious and unguarded. If we're traveling, he'll inform friends and family where we are, where we're going, and who we're going with. For him, sharing what we're doing is part of enjoying the experience, and I try to respect that. But even that level of sharing is *a lot* for me. Every time he does it, I still cringe. Why do people need to know where we're having dinner? I'm not worried that someone is coming to get us, but nobody needs that much information about my life. That's just how I'm wired now.

Even as a married couple, Keion and I are still trying to adapt to my need for caution. For instance, I love traveling, but when Keion and I go on vacation I'm fine if it's just him, or him and our kids. I don't need more than that. I've taken my bubble on the road. But sometimes he'll say, "Let's invite some other couples." My defenses go up immediately. It's difficult for him because he knows I need to choose who can travel with us. Keion can hang with anybody and have a fun time and relax, but I need to know I can let my hair down and have a good time without seeing it on someone's YouTube channel.

But I think he's started to see that we don't need to share *every-thing*. I don't think he had any idea how toxic social media could be until he saw the waters I swim in. But that's only part of the reason he's changed his stance. The other part is that—and there's no other way to put this—culturally, Black people will "count your money for you." Sometimes, when Black folks become aware of what you do, how you do it, and what you have, they start calculating what you're worth—and occasionally, what they can get from you. I don't like that. I don't like people in my pockets.

For example, let's say you take a trip to France. Some Black people will try to figure out how much it costs for you to take that trip, and from there, figure out if you're rich or not. I don't care if people assume I have a lot of money. But when they make comments like, "It must be nice to be able to afford to just stay on the road the way you do," or "I haven't seen this car. Do you have more than one car?," I can tell they're calculating my net worth. To be fair, ninety-nine percent of the people who do this are harmless, but it's that last one percent I worry about.

Another bubble rule I have is that people don't become trust-worthy by association. Everyone has to earn their way into my bubble, and it doesn't matter if they're family. Do you know how many people are burned by a cousin who doesn't like them or by a jealous sibling who tweets something inappropriate? Nobody gets a free pass.

I have a girlfriend in my bubble, and we've known each other since we were teenagers. We don't talk every day, and I don't share everything with her. But she knows all my most sensitive personal information, the things nobody else has access to. If anything goes bad with me, she's the one to call. I trust her with everything.

Also, people can be close professional colleagues or fun to hang out with and still not belong inside the bubble. There are people I've worked with for years on *Basketball Wives* who have never even been to my home. It doesn't mean I don't like them, just that I don't need them any closer than they already are. If you're on the outside, I might get along perfectly well with you. We might work together beautifully, and I might enjoy your company. But you're never going to know my personal business or come inside my home and see me with my guard down.

Does that seem lonely? It is, sometimes. But it also makes me feel safe and secure. I'm on the move constantly, and when I finally stop working, taking meetings, and making decisions, I need a safe space where I can recharge. I don't need someone all up in my business, and I don't want to waste time that I could spend with my husband or my children putting out fires and dealing with drama because someone shared something they shouldn't have. Inside the bubble, I can relax and be myself.

Even with a force field around my personal life, I'm able to maintain my relationships because I don't turn being inside my bubble into a reward, and I don't turn being excluded from it into a punishment. I don't go to the *Basketball Wives* set on a Friday and choose the cast members and crew I want to invite back to my place for a party. Building a bubble while staying friends with the people outside means not broadcasting that you have a bubble in the first place. Let people think what they will.

. . .

One of the things that makes my privacy bubble possible is that I take other people's privacy as seriously as I take my own. You can't expect people to safeguard your privacy if you won't safeguard theirs. If I trust you, and you are part of the inner circle, I'll take your secrets to my grave. What happens in the bubble stays in the bubble.

That's why when I sat down to think about the kind of book I wanted to write, I rejected the idea of a *Basketball Wives* tell-all. A lot of the women on that show have been my friends for years. Some of them are like sisters to me. For me to go behind their backs would be a betrayal.

While I was working on this book, one of the ladies was a guest on a podcast, and she told the hosts that I had provoked her to fight with a particular girl. This woman is well-known for being willing to fight on reality TV. She's combative and volatile; that's just who she is. On the podcast, she claimed I had shown her footage of this woman talking trash about her, making her angry so she would lose it the next time she saw her in person.

What this woman was talking about had happened about eight years earlier. Yes, I did show her the footage she was talking about— because she asked me to. She had taken me aside and said, "Shaunie, if you hear or see something that someone is saying about me, please don't just sit on it. Have my back. That's all I ask." There were only two women on the show at that time that I had that kind of relationship with: her and Evelyn. They both asked me to let them know if anyone was talking trash about them. When I saw that this other woman was having a go at my friend, I told her about it.

She didn't really care that this other girl (who neither of us had ever met) was talking about her. She cared that it gave her a juicy reality-TV moment. But eight years later, keeping my word had become "Shaunie provoked me." I still refused to speak up and contradict the story, because it wasn't going to make my life better to clap back at her and make her look like a liar or a drama queen. I'm obligated to protect her privacy.

You might be saying, "I wouldn't want to live that way." If you are, I understand. Not everyone can, and not everyone should. I don't want my kids to feel like they have to be as hyper-protective as I am. That's why I've taught them how to be careful on social media, to be smart about what they share, and to insist that people earn their trust. Myles is *over* social media. He's an entrepreneur and investor, and he uses Twitter mostly for stock tips and business communications. My older kids use social media mostly for business, for sponsorships, and things they're contracted to post about. Even my oldest daughter, Mimi, only really posts for sponsorships or something she's promoting. The novelty has worn off.

The kids are learning that the fewer people you have in your business, the easier life is. When Shareef signed with the NBA's G League (the association's official developmental league), he got a contract for the most money he'd ever made in his life. I told him, "No one needs to know how much money you make." The team posted on social media that he'd signed a six-figure deal, and I told him, "Say nothing. If your grandmother asks you how much your contract is for, politely decline to answer." People don't need to know that sort of information.

Still, I can't see my kids building bubbles of their own, and that's okay. They haven't been through what I've been through. But for me, after all this time, being in the bubble is a way of life. I'm always careful now. Everyone is on the outside until they prove they belong on the inside. That's the way it has to be. Once you lose your privacy, it's gone for good.

CHAPTER 10

I'M NOT SLEEPING,
I'M WORRYING WITH
MY EYES CLOSED

Part of the reason I obsess over privacy is because I'm a parent, and parenting these days is scary as hell. Predators and identity thieves on social media, mass shootings, pandemics, and then add the other fears that come with being the parent of Black children . . . it's a lot to process. Believe me, having a successful TV show doesn't shield me from lying awake at night hoping my daughter Amirah is safe, or praying that my son Shaqir doesn't get pulled over by a white police officer having a bad night. Fear and worry are just parts of my life that I have to manage, and that hasn't changed since most of my children are grown and no longer live with me.

When Amirah was eighteen, she went off to Louisiana State University for college and to play basketball. This made sense because her father went to LSU, and our son Shareef did as well. But it was also 2020, in the depths of the pandemic, when everybody was scared to death and didn't know how to keep life going while trying to stay safe. Mimi got to the university, but then the fall semester started with the entire school in lockdown, and the isolation really did a number on my little girl's mental health.

I had never worried about my children's mental health before this. When I was growing up, mental health was simply not discussed at home or school. It just wasn't on our radar. If I felt sad or hopeless about something, I didn't tell my parents I was depressed or claim I had a mental health issue, because I didn't know what those things were back then. If I had said something to them, they would have responded with, "How could you possibly be depressed? What do you have to be depressed about? You have no bills to pay. You have no problems. Now get back in your room and finish your homework."

I don't blame my parents for that. They became parents in a different age. There was no internet or social media, so there was no cyberbullying or body shaming—at least not by a mob of strangers. I didn't really experience racism as a child, even though I went to school with predominantly white classmates. There were just what we think of as the "normal" pressures of childhood: fitting in, dealing with crushes and breakups, and the familiar kind of bullying, where a kid calls you names or threatens to kick your ass.

I experienced the last one. My dad was one of those parents who, while he discouraged violence, also told us we should defend ourselves. He didn't condone us starting fights, but if we were being bullied, he wanted us to handle our business. "Listen," he would say, "if someone puts their hands on you, you have all the right in the world to defend yourself, and you had better win." I had two fights during my whole time in school. One was in middle school, with a boy who put his hands on me. We were playing soccer and I beat him, and he got upset and pushed me. No big deal.

In high school, I got into it with a girl who didn't like me because her boyfriend liked me. She wanted to fight me, and I was terrified of her, because I was a freshman, and she was a senior and she was way bigger than I was. She was also one of those girls who would fight everybody. I told my mom what was happening, and she said, "Well, that girl better not put her hands on you, but you're going to school tomorrow." Well, that was a great comfort. What I wanted her to say was, "Baby, you can stay home until this is all over. I'll get your homework from your teachers." In the end, I went to school, and the other girl and I never ended up fighting. So, while she had a beef with me, thankfully it never really evolved into anything physical.

In 2020, we were all dealing with this unprecedented crisis that left us isolated and frightened. Stuck in her dorm, lonely and cut off from her family and friends, Mimi was having an especially tough time. She wrote about her experience, and has allowed me to share some of it:

> I walked on at LSU. The beginning was smooth sailing with work-outs. They were hard, but I enjoyed them. Fast-forward to our first tournament in Vegas. We had two games, and I did not play in either of them. Now, mind you, my expectations were not to come to LSU and start or get a lot of playing time. I knew I had to improve, but I'm not going to lie, not playing in those two games got to me. I even had to deal with the aftermath of what people had to say about me not getting in the game: "Oh, she's probably not that good." It got to me once SEC [Southeastern Conference] play

started. I was told I wouldn't be able to play—something with SEC rules and me being a walk-on. I don't really know. I was still confused on why, game after game, I had to deal with what people said about me. It was always negative.

That season was really tough for me. I went from working really hard and practicing to not. I started to think of so many negative things. I started to feel as if I wasn't wanted there, and that they only let me on the team because of my dad. I felt as if I wasn't good enough to be there. I had no motivation or confidence. I felt so alone and like I just wasted a lot of time.

When I read that, it broke my heart. But I turned around almost immediately, because I found out that my incredible daughter had started her own student mental health platform on Instagram called Athlete Escape. This is what she wrote about it:

I started a mental health platform called Athlete Escape, mainly for student athletes, but everyone has my support, athlete or not. I started this platform because I really want to help others become aware of their mental health and well-being. For a while now, I have struggled with many aspects of bad mental health due to many reasons, one being the sport I played and the experience I had in college. I never really wanted to talk about it because I was afraid of what others would say. Now I know how important it is to speak up and get help. I know there are student athletes who have gone or are going through the same thing as me and are afraid to speak up. So I'm using my platform to create a safe space for those student athletes.

I learned about all this when Mimi came home at the end of the basketball season. During the school year, I went to Baton Rouge quite often to visit her and Shareef, but Mimi always discouraged me from coming on weekends because even though the team was playing, she wasn't. But Mimi being Mimi—she's a happy, silly young lady who's laughing all the time—led me to believe everything was fine. She would say things like, "Oh Mom, you know, next year I'll get some playing time, it's okay." I would ask her how workouts were going, and they were great. Everything was great.

Well, my daughter was playing me. Things weren't great. She wasn't talking about the pain and isolation. Then she came home and seemed a little down. It took a few days for me to chip away at what was really going on, because Mimi is not a complainer. Finally, she told me she didn't want to go back to playing. She would go back to LSU, but she didn't want to go back to the basketball team. At first I thought it was about playing time, and I told her she was sure to play more as a sophomore, because some of the girls were going to graduate. But that didn't seem to lift her spirits. I nudged and pried a little more, and she finally broke down and told me what her experience had been like.

I was appalled and furious. I could understand some homesickness, that was normal. But my baby had been singled out and bullied until she felt completely alone, a feeling made worse by the enforced isolation of COVID. Understand that for most of the school year, the campus was empty. If you were a student-athlete, you had to be there to train and work out with the team, but otherwise, you were in your dorm room attending classes on Zoom. Mimi's freshman year—a time that's supposed to be about new roommates, parties, study groups, and staying up late—consisted of her going to classes on her computer in her dorm, alone, and then spending the rest of the time alone. When she did go to practice or games, she was singled out for abuse. No wonder she didn't want to go back!

I was ready to fight for my daughter, but she didn't need me to. Today, she attends Texas Southern University here in Houston (as does Shaqir), and she's working every day on her mental health. What amazes me is that she didn't blame anyone for her troubles. Instead, she'd say, "It's nobody's fault, Mom. We'll get through it." Plus, she started her platform to try and help others, and I couldn't be prouder of her. But what's even more impressive is that she's thinking beyond basketball. One day she said to me, "I want to do more with my life than basketball. What do you think I should do with myself?" I was thinking, *How did you get so wise, child?*

I still worry about her mental health, but not as much as I used to. She's strong and brave, and I know she's taking care of things.

I sleep a little easier because I know my kids learned all the important lessons when they were growing up. Like my mother and father, I was a strict parent. You didn't even think about breaking my rules. For instance, I trust my children to drink responsibly because they learned from me that the alternative was unacceptable. Not every family is that way. I went to Shareef's high school graduation and saw a young lady carrying what looked like a little gift bag. But when she walked past me, I looked in her bag and saw a big bottle of Tito's vodka. She and her girlfriends were going to get wasted after graduation.

That would never have happened with my kids. Of course, they weren't angels either. One day back when Myles was a freshman at Santa Monica High School, I came home early. He and a white friend were hanging out in our little guesthouse, and as I walked up our driveway, I could smell weed. I went in the house; no weed smell there. But when I went to the guesthouse and opened the door—whew! The smoke billowed out. Myles and his friend were so high they didn't even know how to react. They just stared, like two deer in headlights. I couldn't even reprimand my son at the time because he wasn't following my words.

I had to let Myles sober up. It was sort of funny, because the two of them were talking about the random stuff you talk about when you're high. But I didn't laugh because I was furious with my son. After I sent the other kid home, I said, "What were you thinking about?"

My son decided this was the right time to give me a speech about how smoking marijuana helps you focus. If I really wanted him to become a better student and do better schoolwork, I should support his pot consumption because Johnny's parents and Timmy's parents and everybody else's parents at Santa Monica High were letting their kids smoke weed to treat their ADHD. I just sat there, listening calmly as my fourteen-year-old delivered this outrageous argument with a straight face.

After he was finished, I said, "Well, honey, here's the thing. There's a huge difference between Johnny's dad and mom and me. Johnny also tells his parents to fuck off, and if you ever said that to me, you would be going to school without your front teeth. Johnny can do some things in that household that you will never be able to do in mine. So, let's just take Johnny off the table. You're never going to justify smoking weed to do better on a test." We never had a problem with weed in the house again.

The other area where I watched my kids like a hawk was sex. I told my boys that there were girls who would "put themselves in certain situations to achieve an outcome." My sons are athletes in their own right, and they are the children of a famous, wealthy father. I reminded them that one of the most common things ambitious young men do to wreck their dreams is to get some young woman pregnant. If that seems alarmist, that's because you don't know some of the things parents have said to me about their daughters.

When Shareef was a star basketball player at his high school, more than one mom said something to me like, "My daughter's in love with your son. Wouldn't it be great if they could go out or something? Wouldn't it be great if they could be together forever?" No ma'am, because my son barely knows your daughter, and that's creepy. Why would anyone say that about two sophomores in high school? I want my sons to live and have experiences. I want my daughters to be the strong women I know they can be. I don't want them to be parents before they're ready.

I see young ladies all the time who are obviously in training to land a rich husband, and some of them have moms who are helping them get there! When my boys lived at home, mothers would sometimes drop their daughters off at my house without ever talking to me or asking if anybody was home. Their parents didn't even walk them to the door. It was like DoorDash, only for teenage sex. I called the girls an Uber and sent them home.

Don't get me wrong; I was never opposed to my kids having friends over. If Me'arah wants to have a couple of her girlfriends over, that's fine. If one of my sons is hanging out at the house and wants to invite some buddies over to watch a ballgame, it's all good. Even if one of my kids invites a friend to come over with his girlfriend and another girl, and they're just planning to hang out in the living room and watch TV, that's totally fine with me. But I have three rules:

- I want to know the kids.
- I always keep one eye and one ear open.
- A guy and girl are never allowed to go somewhere private alone.

When Mimi and Me'arah both lived at home and were planning to stay at a girlfriend's house, I would always ask if that friend had brothers. If she did, I would ask the parent in charge, "Will your sons be around?" If the answer was yes, I'd ask, "Will you be around?" If there wouldn't be adult supervision, then we would be rescheduling that sleepover. Boys will be boys, and girls will be girls. That doesn't change.

My mom likes to say, "When children are small, they pull at your hem. When they get older, they pull at your heart." One way to translate that is as your kids age, your fears change. Before they're even born, you're praying they'll have ten fingers and ten toes and that they won't get sick. Then you worry about them doing well in school and making friends. But those fears are nothing compared to the fears when they get old enough to go out into the world.

I try to not be consumed by fear and worry, but I pray about my kids all day. I could be driving across Houston to a meeting or to have lunch with Keion and suddenly be saying to myself, "God please build a hedge of protection around my children at all times." Anything will set my heart racing and imagining the worst. In August 2022, while I was working on this book, a woman in a Mercedes plowed through an intersection in the Windsor Hills neighborhood of Los Angeles at about one hundred miles an hour, killing six people—including a pregnant woman—and injuring nine more. It was awful, and it was four minutes from my parents' house. Immediately, I thought, *God, spare my children, please.*

It's worse now that all my kids are driving. There was a point when Myles was turning sixteen that I said to myself, "I can't wait until he gets his license. He can start taking himself to school and games." With every one of my kids, I was so happy when they finally got their driver's license. I could finally hang up my chauffeur's cap. But now we live in Texas, where it seems like everyone is angry all the time. There is road rage everywhere here, and everyone in Texas seems to carry a gun. Having my kids driving in that kind of environment scares the hell out of me.

In Houston, some time ago, there was a fender bender between a little Toyota Corolla and a pickup truck. The driver at fault was a young woman who had a toddler in the back seat of the Toyota, and I assume she didn't have insurance, because she tried to drive away from the accident. That's against the law, obviously. But when she started to drive away, the girlfriend of the pickup driver pulled out a gun and started shooting at the Corolla! She didn't know there was a toddler in the back, but that doesn't matter. Shooting at a car like that is insane.

I have five beautiful Black children. All but one of them has left home and gone out on their own, and they've done that in a country that is hostile to their survival. Myles started driving when he was in high school, and even back then I had to tell him how to stay alive. "Make sure your hands are visible at ten and two so the officer can see them," I said. "Stay calm. Don't argue with the officer." Although it seems these days that even following those rules isn't enough to keep a young Black man safe. That's what terrifies me.

But for all my worrying about traffic stops and road rage, the scariest experience of my life was when Shareef had open heart surgery. It was August 2018, and after signing to attend UCLA, he was doing summer workouts with the basketball team. He had also been wearing a heart monitor after telling the medical staff that he "felt funny" during some practices, but we figured that was just a precaution. Nothing would come of it, right?

I was out of town with a friend, and the night before I was scheduled to come home, the UCLA athletic trainer called me and said, "Hey, could you come into the office?" I told him I was out of town. Could I come Monday? "No. I think you should come straight from the airport after you land. I don't care what time it is. You and Shareef should come to the office." Now I was in a panic, but he wouldn't give me any additional information.

I landed the next day and headed straight for UCLA. I met Shareef, and he didn't know what was going on any more than I did. We headed for the athletic department, and they showed us into a conference room . . . and I couldn't believe how many doctors were at this long table. I didn't know anyone except for the trainer, who looked like he wanted to cry. Shaquille was there via FaceTime. Now I was on the verge of a panic attack. Fortunately, they didn't waste time. We sat down and the lead UCLA physician pulled up a picture of a heart on a screen, and they explained to us that Shareef had a congenital heart defect.

He had been born, they said, with a coronary artery that was in the wrong location. When he exercised and his heart expanded with the exertion, it would compress the artery and reduce the flow of blood from his heart to other parts of his body. The good news was, this was a treatable condition, and once it was fixed, it wouldn't come back. Shareef could go on about his life, be an athlete, play in the NBA, and do all the things he dreamed of doing. The shocking news was, he would need open-heart surgery to fix it.

After the words "open-heart surgery" were spoken, I stopped being able to hear anything else. Shaquille said something and I had no idea what it was. The doctors started talking about the defect and how they would repair it, but my brain was stuck on repeat: *My eighteen-year-old baby boy needs open heart surgery . . .*

Shareef and I just needed to get out of that room. We excused ourselves, went outside, and headed for the parking lot, but settled for collapsing on a bench along the path. I held my boy and let him cry, and I cried with him for what felt like forty-five minutes. I don't think there is anything worse than being a parent and not being able to do anything about what's happening to your child. You're used to being able to offer the solution, but I had nothing to give Shareef besides my support and empty words like, "It's going to be okay."

The one thing I could do for my son was empower him. I told Shareef that having the surgery was his decision. I would round up the best doctors and trainers, and we would get the best advice possible, but it would be his call. He could choose not to get the operation, and he would be able to live with the condition. But he wouldn't be able to be an athlete anymore. No college or pro program would ever clear him to play because of the potential legal liability. He would also have to monitor his heart rate for the rest of his life. Or, he could get the surgery and accept the risks involved, which ranged from infection to death.

That's a lot to put on an eighteen-year-old, but this was a decision Shaquille and I could not make for him. I remember thinking, *Either he chooses the surgery and I'm going to lose my mind until he's out of recovery, or he doesn't get it and I'm going to lose my mind for the rest of my life, worrying about him every minute of every day.* But I said nothing about my fears. I had no right to burden him with my anxiety.

He chose to go ahead with the surgery. From the time we got the news until the surgery date was about two months, and I don't think I stopped crying the entire time. I've never cried that much in my life. Every time I thought about my boy on the operating table, every time a song about mothers or sons came on, every time somebody talked to me about the surgery, I fell apart. It was too much.

Then the day came. It was the most stressful day of my life. When they wheeled Shareef away to go into that surgical suite, it haunted me that he was going in there all alone. All I wanted was to be with him and hold his hand. I didn't want to see the surgery, because I knew I would not be able to handle that. But if I were in an adjacent room, I could stick my arm into the OR and hold his hand and he would know I was nearby. It's amazing where your mind goes in a situation like that. In my head, my baby was in a room full of doctors and nurses and frightening machines and people saying things he couldn't understand, and he needed his mother. Of course, in reality, he'd gotten presurgical sedation so he was relaxed and sleepy.

Shareef was in the hospital for a total of five days, from December 13 to 17. He did so well that he was up and walking a little less than twenty-four hours after the surgery. No complications. During all that time, I only left once, and my mom had to practically kick me out to make that happen. She came to the hospital one day and told me to go to our hotel to take a real shower, as I had been using the hospital room shower. "Please," she said, "I need you to take a breather, get out of this hospital, go to the hotel, get a real hot shower, change into some clothes that are gonna make you feel a little better, and get some fresh air." My mother was worrying about me, just like I was worrying about my kids, and she was taking charge, which was wonderful. I did what she said.

Apart from that brief break, I stayed by Shareef's side and did not leave the hospital until he did. After he was discharged, we all spent two days in the hotel just to make sure he got his pain meds, follow-ups with doctors, and things like that. After he came home, the process of his recovery put constant demands on me, but I was ready to care for my boy. I set alarms on my phone for all the medication he had to take throughout the day and night. I learned how to manage his pain medication wisely because he definitely needed it. I learned a lot about physically caring for someone and developed so much respect for nurses and in-home caregivers.

I also spent a lot of time monitoring Shareef's emotional and mental state. The doctors had warned me that open-heart surgery patients often feel "different" afterward. One doctor told me to think of it this way: Their heart has literally been touched by someone else's hands, and that's not normal. It changes them, and often makes them more emotional. After his surgery, I watched my son go from shutting down to being deeply emotional. He's had great emotional and moral strength his whole life, but the experience really brought that to the surface. Today, nearly six years after the surgery, he's an even more deeply caring person. Today, if he hears through the grapevine that somebody is having open-heart surgery or anything related to it—even if he has never met the person—he will find that person, so he can talk to them and encourage or help them. Because he's been there. He knows how scary it is and he goes out of his way to be supportive and helpful.

Even his siblings call Shareef "Dad" sometimes because he's so protective. He always knows where everybody is. He always knows what's going on. If somebody has a game or a performance and he can't make it, he'll always take the time to call and ask, "How was your game? How many points did you score?" or "How did the show go?" It's like the surgery gave him the wisdom of someone twenty years older. It's incredible to see. He's become an amazing man, and I'm not just saying that because he's mine. I imagine he thinks about the surgery occasionally, because how could an experience like that not affect you in some capacity? I'll go back to that memory sometimes myself. But if it's rattled him, he doesn't show it. He's a lot braver than his mom.

Remember "the Talk"? You probably had it with your mother, or maybe your father. When we were kids "the Talk" meant sitting down with your mom or dad and having an incredibly awkward conversation about sex, pregnancy, and birth control. If you're raising Black children, "the Talk" is different. It's about how to behave when you're in a situation where you're around a white person who seems ready to turn an innocent encounter into something racist and even potentially violent.

Now, "the Talk" is about warning your Black teenage child who's just gotten their driver's license—and who should get to be excited about finally being able to drive—and walking them through the steps they need to follow in case they get pulled over by the police so they don't get shot in the back and die. It's heartbreaking to have to sit down across from your beautiful dark-skinned child and explain that if a white woman raises her voice in a Walmart, it's best to be respectful, stay calm, and say nothing, because she might be a "Karen," a high-strung woman who might be ready to weaponize her whiteness against Black people.

I have a niece, and when she was just nine years old I taught her that when we go to public places she should keep one eye out for Karens. Was I overreacting in teaching a fourth grader about out-of-control white ladies who call the police on Black children who sell bottled water door-to-door or show up to swim at the neighborhood pool? I don't think so, but I would rather overreact and have the kids in my family know to keep their heads on a swivel and have the sense to avoid trouble.

While I was working on this book, Keenan Anderson, the cousin of Black Lives Matter cofounder Patrisse Cullors, died of cardiac arrest after being tased multiple times by Los Angeles police officers after a traffic collision. The thirty-one-year-old teacher was heard screaming, "Help, they're trying to kill me" and "Please, don't do this."

Don't tell me I'm overreacting.

Of course, I can't spend all my time worrying. To control my anxiety and make sure I can sleep, I rely on social media. On an average day I might talk with three of my five kids. To check on the other two, I'll go to their social media feeds and check the last time they posted. They post less often than they used to, but they're still on pretty regularly. If they posted two hours earlier that they were going to the movies with friends, I'm good. But if I'm going to bed at 11 p.m., and they last posted at eleven that morning, they're going to get a call from me: "Hey, just checking on you." I just need to know they're okay, and then I can leave them alone, relax, and get a good night's sleep. That's what I need to do to fall asleep each night. To know that my children are safe and accounted for.

One thing I try not to do is make my kids feel any more anxious about their safety than I have to. I want them to be cautious and smart, not fearful. One day, back when he was nineteen, Shaqir called me and sounded really scared. He said, "Mom, I need to go to the emergency room. My chest hurts." As you can imagine, that set off alarm bells, especially when I'd already had one child have open-heart surgery.

I said, "Baby, have you done anything that might have hurt your chest?" He told me he'd been weight training for two weeks getting ready for basketball, and that the bench press bar had hit his chest hard the day before. It seemed likely to me that he'd bruised his sternum or strained the ligaments between his sternum and rib cage—a painful injury, but not serious, and certainly not a reason to go to the ER. But Shaqir wanted to go to the hospital. I said, "Let me throw my shoes on. I could be there in twenty to twenty-five minutes."

"No, I need to go now." In fact, he had already called Amirah, who lived on the sixtieth floor of his building, to drive him. Sighing, I told him to go to urgent care—*not* the ER—and that I would meet him there. When I arrived, Shaqir was already checked in, on an IV, hooked up to monitors, and looking pretty scared. This was about Shareef, of course. In his mind, his chest pain might be a symptom of the same arterial deformity his brother had.

When I walked in, the first person I saw was Mimi, who just rolled her eyes at me. What are the odds that a nineteen-year-old athlete in perfect health would have a heart attack? I figured they were pretty slim. The nurses took X-rays, which confirmed what I had been think-ing: Shaqir had a bruised sternum, probably from the bar hitting him in the chest. The doctor explained all this to him, but Shaqir was still saying he felt weak.

Now the doctor became more concerned. He said to Shaqir, "Is this settling, what I'm telling you? Because you don't seem settled with it. Are you not telling us something?" The doctor was second-guessing himself and considering calling a cardiologist, so I stepped in. "This kid can get up and leave," I said. "He's fine." And with that, we checked out and went home.

When we got outside, I told Shaqir that he needed to learn to distinguish problems that were a two on the emergency scale from problems that were a legitimate ten. I knew he was sore, and that what happened to his brother had him spooked, but I didn't want him sending us all into a panic over nothing. He'll have plenty of time to do that after he has children of his own.

In a few days his chest was fine.

Like many of us, the pandemic gave me a whole new reason to worry. When everything locked down in 2020, I ended up with the girls in Houston, where we had just moved, and the boys ended up with Shaquille in Orlando. That was a strange arrangement, not least because Shaquille and I had different attitudes about what *lockdown* meant.

The girls and I had our bikes, and we would ride around our neighborhood, but it was just us. When I would FaceTime with the boys, I could see that the house was full of people. I had my "girl cave" with my daughters, my sons had their man cave with their father—the gym and basketball court and all the rest—and that was fine. But I was not okay with a house full of strangers, any of whom could be carrying COVID.

I said to Shaquille, "You do understand we're in the middle of a pandemic right now, right?" His reply? "We're locked down. Everybody that comes in is locked in." That wasn't reassuring, but thank God, everybody stayed safe. Shareef didn't get COVID until he went to LSU.

While I was working on this book, Me'arah went back to in-person classes for the first time since she was in eighth grade. I was *not* happy about it. I know that it was tough for her to spend the first two years of high school going to classes via Zoom and not being able to see her friends. I know being at school in person is a thousand times better for learning, socializing, mental health, everything. Then I think about how much safer it felt when she was home with me. We moved around a lot because of *Basketball Wives*, so it was easier for her to continue attending school online because she could travel with me, and it wouldn't affect her grades.

After COVID restrictions were lifted and we stopped moving

around, she was ready to go back to school and play basketball, and I didn't blame her. What sixteen-year-old girl wants to be cooped up in her house with her mom all the time? But the closer it got, the more anxious I became. She went back and thrived, but I still felt uneasy. I want her to have the full high school experience just like her siblings did. I want her to be a normal kid, go to class, participate in extracurricular activities, go to the senior prom, and graduate. She shouldn't have to pay the price for my fear. Still, I drive her to school every day. I like that time with her. She'll be the last one to leave home, and I'm trying to enjoy and prolong every moment I can get with her.

I know that part of my worrying and fear come from how I was raised. I didn't have much of a social life in high school because my father's idea of protecting me was keeping me at home. I didn't go to my prom or any other high school dances because he was worried something bad would happen. He wanted to know that I was in my room or in the living room with him and my mom. I could go to sleepovers, but only at cousins' houses. That was my dad's way of controlling his own anxiety.

I loved my father, but he imposed his fear on me. I like to think I've done better with my kids. They've played sports, gone to college, met new people, and had adventures. Now most of them live on their own and they're still alive. But I won't stop worrying, not until I'm a gray-haired old lady . . . and probably not even then.

CHAPTER 11

THE LOVE OF MY LIFE

After my divorce, I was busy putting my life back together, building *Basketball Wives*, and raising my kids. But I also wanted to get out and date other men. I had married when I was twenty-eight, but because of my strict upbringing I hadn't dated a great deal before getting married and having kids. Now I was forty, experienced at life, looking and feeling great, and I really wanted to get back into the dating scene. I didn't expect to find my soulmate, but I did want to have some fun.

The first guy I dated was a lot younger than I was, which was perfect. I didn't know if I was ready for another committed relationship, but I was interested in having a good time, and this guy and I did a lot of fun things together. Because I had become a mother at twenty-two, I'd missed out on the single life a lot of my peers had enjoyed, and I was keen to make up for lost time. I became the woman who stayed out until two in the morning!

However, the difference in maturity levels between me and this guy drove me crazy. I wasn't interested in teaching a grown man how to be a man, so that relationship got old fast. At that point, I decided I just wanted a casual boyfriend, nothing more. I was not interested in a serious relationship. After that, I dated a few more guys who were just okay, and that was fine. Then I met a guy I thought was a real catch—not necessarily marriage material, but someone I could have committed to for the long term.

He lived in another state, and after we had dated for about six months, I went to visit him at what he had *told me* was his house. Yeah, you're with me. When I got to the address he had given me, I noticed there were no pictures of him on the walls. I thought, *Well, that's normal, because what single guy has photos of himself on the walls?* I found out later that it wasn't even his house. It was just the listing of a Realtor friend of his. The guy was a complete fraud. Everything he'd told me about who he was and what he did was a lie. Who does that? Why would a man in his forties put on such an act?

Needless to say, that was the end of that relationship. I never heard from him again, and good riddance. After that, I went cold turkey on men for a while. To me, the dating pool was full of pee, and I wanted no part of it. My kids were happy and healthy, I was busy with my show and my career, and that was enough for me. I gave up on dating for the time being. So, when I found Keion, I wasn't even looking. But that's usually when lightning strikes, isn't it?

After my divorce, if you had told me I would end up married to a minister and would be the first lady of a church, I would have laughed in your face. But here we are. My marriage to Keion is proof positive that the best way to make God laugh is to say "Never."

Several years ago, I was on a panel at a single women's conference here in Houston, and Keion Henderson was the moderator. I didn't know anything about him, and barely said two words to him outside the panel. Some time later, a gentleman who was a mutual friend called me and said, "Remember that guy, he was on this panel, and you were on this panel . . . ?" I said yes, vaguely. The friend told me that Keion was newly single, and he thought we would like each other.

This mutual friend has known me for years—when I was married, when I was divorced, when I was dating some losers, and more. He knew what I wanted in a man and what I couldn't stand. I thought, *Why not?* Then something occurred to me. "Wait, isn't he a pastor?"

"Yeah."

I laughed. "Oh, Lord no." I asked my friend why he thought a pastor would be a good match for me, because he knew that I liked to have a lot of fun. Dating a pastor seemed like a bad fit. If we got into a relationship, wouldn't my whole life have to revolve around church? I love God and I grew up going to church with my mother, but I didn't want to eat, sleep, and breathe either one. But this friend insisted we would be a good match and talked me into giving it a chance. One date. Fine. How much trouble could I get into on one date?

My friend gave Keion my number, and he called me. I was living in Los Angeles at the time, and he lived in Houston, and with my schedule it took a couple of months to figure out when we could meet. So, we talked on the phone a little bit and that was nice. He seemed cool and normal. But I was still thinking, *He's a pastor. He's gonna be boring.* Long story short, he had to preach in California, far from Los Angeles, but he arranged a return flight out of LAX so we could have dinner in L.A. Unfortunately, I already had dinner plans with friends, so I called him and said, "I could swing by and say hello after I'm finished with dinner." Looking back, I was so indifferent I still can't believe he hung in there.

I ended up meeting him at around 10 p.m. at his hotel near the airport, and we sat in the restaurant and chatted. Strategically, I ordered a margarita. I didn't want him to have any illusions about me. I love a good cocktail and am *going* to have one every now and then. Then he ordered one, too, and I thought, *Okay, that's good.*

We talked for about three hours, and it was effortless. Do you know those conversations that just jump from one topic to another naturally, with no tension or awkward silences? It was like that. Finally, at about one o'clock in the morning, the hotel bar closed and they kicked us out. We moved to chairs in the lobby and kept talking for what must have been another three hours. All I know is that by the time we got done, the sky was starting to turn light. It was the best night I had ever had, and all we did was talk. Finally, I said, "I guess I should probably go home." He had an eight o'clock flight. He walked me to my car, I got in, and I drove home. Then I said to myself, *Dammit, I really like him.*

In the following days, the more I thought about Keion, the more excited I got. Everything about him was perfect to me. He was more handsome than I remembered him being. He was kind, articulate, intelligent, had a relaxed confidence about him, and seemed content just to be with me, talking all night. I couldn't wait to see him again.

That was all she wrote. We just kept talking to each other. Because of COVID-19, we didn't see each other again for a while, but we talked all the time on the phone and developed a wonderful bond. We connected. We shared secrets. We became intimate, even though we weren't, you know, *intimate*. By the time we were able to spend time together in person again, I had fallen in love with him.

Of course, that's not the whole story. I knew I had to consider how my children would feel about this man. Would they expect him to be a father? Would they resent him as someone who was replacing their father? Well, I worried for nothing. My kids *adore* Keion. Even better, each of them has their own relationship with him, and I don't even have to be involved. They text and call him all the time. It's amazing.

I don't know how he did it, but I think it's because he was patient and let my kids come to him when they were ready, instead of forcing himself on them. He's a great father to his daughter, and it showed. He was there when they needed him if they needed him. When he first came around, Me'arah was just fourteen and she needed a father's presence. Keion was able to sense that she was missing that in her life, so he started going to the gym with her and playing basketball. He played in college, so he knows the game, and they really bonded over that. They have a beautiful relationship.

Shareef and Shaqir were in college and out of the house when Keion and I became serious. But they bonded from a distance, and when we got married, the boys helped Keion dress for the wedding. They have a great relationship, too. They also told me, "Mom, we see that you're happy, and that's all that matters."

Keion loves my kids too, which makes me love him even more. It's not easy to be with someone who has five kids. That could've been an obstacle, but it wasn't, and part of the reason is that I'm blessed with five kids who are just wonderful human beings. They saw right away that Keion is a good strong man of great character, and that he loves me deeply. They trust him, which is why they'll talk with him and get advice about issues and big questions I'm not even involved with.

When we finally got engaged, I went to each of my children and asked them, "How do you feel about this? Is this all right with you?" Every one of them said, "Mom, we're totally happy."

My boys asked, "Mom, what took so long?"

My relationship with Keion has reminded me that substance always beats style. When I met Shaquille, I fell for the charm and the gifts and the dramatic gestures. But that stuff doesn't last. Like me, Keion is divorced, so he knows that type of pain. We both looked for different things this time around. We both wanted physical and sexual attraction, sure, but we also wanted character, confidence, and kindness. We wanted someone who would help us be the best versions of ourselves—who would walk beside us, hand in hand, as we built a life together.

Keion and I found out just how compatible we were in this way during the lead-in to our wedding. We ended up holding our wedding on the island of Anguilla as a three-part special on VH1 called *Shaunie & Keion's Destination "I Do."* You might wonder why I—someone who guards her privacy so carefully and detests drama—would agree to turn my wedding into a very public TV spectacle. Good question. I wish I had a good answer. But it worked because Keion and I work.

Turning the wedding into a TV special was part my idea and part VH1's idea. I wasn't planning on telling them about the wedding, because I knew they would say, "Can you get married on *Basketball*

Wives?" Absolutely not. But I couldn't keep the news from my team at VH1 forever, and when they found out, they wanted to do *something*. Finally, I said, "Maybe it could be a spin-off. I don't want it to be associated with *Basketball Wives*."

The VH1 bigwigs thought about this and then came back with a suggestion: turn the wedding into a three-part special. That seemed reasonable, and I agreed. I was used to producing fourteen or sixteen episodes of a series; how difficult could doing three episodes be?

One episode would be the wedding, obviously. But I had no idea what the other two would be. When I finally figured out what would be in those episodes, everything still sounded pretty easy in my head. All the while, Keion was handling church business and I was handling *Basketball Wives*, but I figured we would get little things done here and there and just find a way to fit it all in. Then it hit me that we were throwing a destination wedding several thousand miles away on a Caribbean island and trying to piece it all together from Houston. This was going to be way harder than we had anticipated.

We had chosen to get married in Anguilla in part because we thought an out-of-the-way location would help us keep the wedding small and simple. Not a lot of folks go to Anguilla. There are only two direct flights per week from the U.S., and if you miss those, you have to fly to nearby St. Maarten and take a boat. We thought we had been so clever, and then we started getting the RSVPs. *Everyone* was excited about coming. This wedding was going to be about five times bigger than we'd imagined!

I got so into planning the wedding that the demands of the TV special became a headache. The production company would call and try to schedule shoots. I didn't have time for shoots; I was planning a wedding! They would ask me to shoot a scene on Wednesday, but that was when we were doing our seating chart. The interruptions were constant. Plus, there's just so much involved in filming, from hair to makeup to wardrobe and more, that it consumed all our time.

Those months of tedious planning and stressful decisions were also a trial by fire for me and Keion. Could we work together and stay friends? Could we listen to each other, delegate, disagree, and come out on the other side still holding hands? *Yes.* People talk about wedding planning as being the woman's job, but Keion participated in everything. We had our meeting with the wedding coordinators together. On the trips where we picked a venue or flowers, we did it together. When the sheer number of small choices to be made—what song did we want to play when we walked down the aisle, what music did we want playing while the guests were being seated?—all became too much, he was incredibly calming.

The details of a wedding are overwhelming under normal circumstances, but when you factor in producers, a crew, and a network all asking questions, you've jumped to crazy. Keion really stepped up here. He knew that with my background in TV that I'm an expert in herding cats: making a list, running through it, and getting things done. But he also knew when to step in and say, "Okay. Two of those things need to come off your list. I'll handle them." God bless the man.

Even with Keion as my calm center, it was tough. At the end of some days I went to bed thinking, *Today was a great day. I completed four entire things. I didn't start them and not finish them. I don't have to go back to them tomorrow.* Other days I would be holding my head in my hands saying, "I don't know what I did today. Did I complete anything?"

The most stressful part of the whole experience was our wedding planner. She was useless. She made big promises, but as the date got closer, she kept saying things like, "I don't know if I'm going to be able to pull this off. Anguilla doesn't have this, and Anguilla doesn't have that. I'm going to have to get this from Chicago and I'm going to have to get that from New York." She kept quoting us higher prices; our budget *tripled*. About three weeks before the wedding, I told Keion, "I can't do this anymore."

Eventually, I fired her, and our wedding ended up being incredible because everyone pitched in and made it happen. People stepped in to take care of things like decor, music, and food and make them happen perfectly. Still, right up to the day before we flew to Anguilla, the wedding was being pieced together. For instance, we had planned to hold a welcome reception to thank our guests for coming, but that was unfinished and unconfirmed. But when we arrived on the island, the resort staff said, "We can do this, don't worry." Those people did a marvelous job throwing a welcome reception and managing all the meaningful details. We lost a wedding planner, but we gained a team.

The other stressful part was the rehearsal. It was the most serious wedding rehearsal I had ever seen because we weren't just making sure the bride and groom knew where they would have the rings, or who would walk down the aisle with whom. We were rehearsing a TV shoot with a crew and equipment that had been transported to Anguilla at considerable expense. Everything had to look exactly like it would on the wedding day. We set up and the crew was filming the rehearsal, which was fine. Then the director started to interrupt, saying things like, "Are we sure we want that there? Can we do it differently because the camera's going to be here, and the lighting will be there?"

I stopped the rehearsal. I gathered the crew together privately and laid down the law. I reminded them that this was not a performance. This was our actual wedding, and we cared more about it being perfect for us and our loved ones than we did about what the crew got for the show. We didn't want the guests to feel like they were extras in a basic cable TV show. They would know we were filming, but I would not allow the cameras and crew to be a distraction. There would be no zooming, moving lights and reflectors, or any of that. I told the camera guys, "You need to become a tree and be still, because if you're still, no one will pay attention to you. I also don't need seven cameras. We only need three."

That was the one time I had to get upset and put my foot down. To their credit, the director, crew, tech guys, and everyone involved respected everything I was saying. I also understood that this was entertainment. It was their job to care more about shots and lighting than to worry about what I needed. They were supposed to push the limit until I pushed back, and when I did, they were completely professional. They made it work. They didn't even talk to me during the ceremony. Honestly, I don't even remember cameras being at the wedding, but my mind was a little preoccupied!

That's how we managed to put on a destination wedding thousands of miles from home for one hundred and eighty people, film the whole thing, and stay sane. I had a vision of what I wanted, and Keion supported that vision and kept us both chill when things got tense. We passed that test with flying colors.

Putting on a big televised wedding is the most public thing I have ever done, and the most private. We had hundreds of people around us—guests, resort staff, TV crew—but the entire affair ended up with just me and Keion looking into each other's eyes as we took our vows to love one another, a private, intimate moment that was just for the two of us.

Because of the wedding special, and because I've been in two very public marriages, I get a lot of questions about relationships. People ask me, "How can I better my relationship with the person I intend to share my life with?" There isn't a one-size-fits-all answer, because every relationship is different, but I think the thing that's missing in many relationships is *intimacy*. Intimacy is a familiarity, friendship, and closeness with the other person. The problem is, we confuse sex and romance with intimacy.

I was having lunch with Keion before we got engaged, and what was supposed to be a one-hour lunch turned into four. At some point in those four hours he said something that shook me. "Intimacy is you seeing into me." He said that we talk about sex, romance, and relationships because those are headline words, but the really challenging work is done in the area of intimacy. If you see into me, and I see into you, we have intimacy, and we have romance, and sex is incredible. If you don't see into me, and I don't see into you, everything is on the surface, and romance is impossible. Sex is meaningless.

I think when you're dating, you shouldn't look for somebody who's great in the bedroom or great at romantic gestures. Look for someone who has the courage to let you see into them and who cares enough to take the time to see into you. If you build your relationship on intimacy and allow romance to be the result of intimacy, sex is wonderful because it's intimate.

When I met Keion, I found out I had been craving real intimacy. I thought I'd had it in my marriage to Shaquille, but while we had romantic gestures and lots of material comforts, we didn't have shared time together. We didn't have that sense of collaborating on a life together. But I know now what real intimacy is. One of the things that makes my intimacy with Keion so strong is that he's fully integrated into the lives of my kids. He's their confidant, friend, and advisor, and they really enjoy each other's company.

The other thing I've learned with Keion is that intimacy means being *partners*. Since our wedding, many people have asked us to talk about our journey together. We did an interview for a new magazine about our relationship, and after they put the video up on their YouTube channel, it got 250 million views in just five days. We thought, *Wow, there's something here.* So, while we will *absolutely not* be producing a reality show about our lives, we will be working on ways to share what we've learned about love and about each other.

When you are with the right man and he loves you the right way, you love him the right way. You adapt to make each other happy. For example, in the past if we went to a hotel, I would live out of my suitcase. Meaning, I wouldn't unpack. Keon unpacks. I used to ask, "Why do you unpack? It's so much work. It's unnecessary." But it drove him nuts that I would live out of my bags, because when it was time for us to go somewhere, I would be tearing my suitcase apart looking for something and yelling things like, "I thought I brought a belt!" or "I know I brought that comb!"

Finally, he couldn't take it anymore. When we would get to a hotel, he would first unpack his suitcase and then he would unpack mine. I thought, *I'm going to start unpacking because that will make him happy.* I get it. I was just being lazy. Now I find myself unpacking my luggage not because he said "Unpack your luggage," but because I know that's something that makes him happy. Now I'm organized and we're on time. That way of loving somebody, and them loving you the right way, makes you want to do things that make each other happy.

Those are the small acts of love that nobody talks about. They're not grand gestures, but they mean a lot. They're little things that you only notice when you really care about someone. Making that small change doesn't cost you anything, but it could mean a lot to your partner.

Keion has brought that kind of real love into my life. I needed a man who would do anything to make me a part of his life and be a part of mine. The love I feel coming from Keion is like no love I've ever felt. It's not roses. It's not material things. It's knowing that this man will do anything to make sure that I know that he loves me every day. It's him putting the effort into getting to know everything about me and learning how to function with me in his life for the rest of his life. I've never had someone invest that kind of time and attention in me.

My dad was my first love, and he showed me what I should expect from a man by being polite and courteous and always treating me like a lady. But having an intimate relationship—learning to communicate with another person, learning how they need to receive love—is something your father can't really teach you. I'm learning those lessons with Keion. After my divorce, my self-esteem and self-confidence were low. Even after I started *Basketball Wives*, I was insecure. I walked around ashamed for a long time. I was embarrassed to be a single mom of five with a failed marriage. But now I know that I *deserve* real, true, life-changing love. And I've found it.

CHAPTER 12

FISH OUT OF WATER

Over the years, there have been a lot of Shaunies. There was the beloved daughter and pageant contestant. The NBA wife. The loving-but-strict mom. The fiercely independent divorcée. The reality show producer and entrepreneur. The TV personality. The sister and friend. Finally, there's the madly-in-love wife. But marrying Keion meant that I also acquired another identity I never could have expected in a million years: first lady of the Lighthouse Church & Ministries in Humble, Texas.

Talk about a role I never thought I would be playing! It was funny—right away, some people thought Keion had "saved" me. I was the Hollywood heathen, and he was going to take me away from my life of sin! What they didn't know was that during my whole childhood I went to a Baptist church with my mom. Growing up, I would be at church twice a week, and all day Sunday. When Keion and I first got together and I went to his church, all these sweet people came up to me and said things like, "I know that you're probably uncomfortable in this space, and it's okay." They tried to teach me the p's and q's and etiquette of church. Eventually I said, "Thank you so much, but I grew up here. My mother was the pianist at our church."

Still, it's been an adjustment. I've spent years becoming the fiercely independent version of Shaunie that I am today, and I'm intensely proud of that. So, it's a little off-putting to suggest that Keion is my white knight, saving me from a godless life that couldn't possibly have been happy because I was single. By this point in the book, you know me well enough to laugh at that idea. I chose to be with Keion because I fell in love with a beautiful man who made me feel seen and loved, and who made me feel even better about myself than I already did. I didn't need anyone to save me or fix me. But I don't mention that to the sweet old ladies at church.

People keep passing judgment, though. I saw a question on Facebook, "Now that Shaunie has married a pastor, will she still do *Basketball Wives*? Because I don't think she should." People were having a conversation about it. I was offended at first, but I understand. People are most comfortable when they can define you—when they can put you in a box. To them, the most comfortable definition for a woman is "wife and mother," not "single mom and TV entrepreneur."

People think they know me because they've seen me on the show for ten years. When Keion and I got together, a lot of people acted like I had been marking time as a TV producer and personality until a man came along to take me away from it all—like they think he's going to tame me. That's ridiculous. He loves every part of me, including the independent, stubborn, strong-willed part. If that makes some people uncomfortable, that's their problem.

In any case, I'm a first lady now, and I'm determined to become my own kind of first lady. People whose lives revolve around the church often have this image of first ladies as not being worldly, but extremely formal and feminine, almost regal. They're living examples whose main purpose is to stand by their man, represent the church, and save souls. I'm sure there are people who think I should give up doing *Basketball Wives* because I'm part of Keion's church. That's not going to happen. I'll find other ways to help my husband and be a good ambassador for the community he's built.

Still, being first lady is awkward. I've tried to get the church staff— who I must say are some of the loveliest people I have ever met—not to call me "first lady," but good luck with that. One day I said, "You guys can just say Shaunie, it's fine. I don't find it disrespectful." Well, I thought somebody was going to have an attack of the vapors. "Oh, no. Oh, God no. That is just . . . we cannot do that. Can you please give us something else?"

Keion laughs about it, because now everybody refers to me as "Lady." They say, "Tell Lady this, tell Lady that." He teases me about it all the time. "You told them not to call you 'First Lady,' " he'll say, "and now they're just trying to figure out what to call you." But he has my back. I do understand because my mother is the same way. The first lady of our church was one of her best friends, and outside of church she was Joan, but in church, or in church settings, Mom always called her Lady Joan. In that setting, it's proper protocol.

In many large Black churches, being first lady is like being royalty. You're pampered and catered to and expected to conduct yourself with class and discretion. I've seen first ladies who sat on a chair that could only be called a throne. Many first ladies eat that up. They're waited on hand and foot and not even allowed to carry anything.

I went somewhere with Keion and there was a first lady seated in a chair. Her hair was long and straight, and when she sat the back of her chair naturally messed it up a little. Every time she stood up, there was a lady behind her who combed her hair back to perfection. I bit my tongue, but later I said to Keion, "Don't ever do that to me. I don't care if my hair is a disaster, do not pull out a comb and fix it in public." Things like that are ridiculous and so extra. Just tell me, "Shaunie, your hair is kind of a mess," and I'll take care of it.

That's who I am. I cringe when people try to wait on me. I don't like being treated like I'm different or more important than anyone else. I'll say, "Please, let me walk to the kitchen and back." I'm an old-fashioned, low-maintenance woman. I love to cook, and I hate anyone fussing over me. But trying to get the folks at Keion's church to embrace the idea of a more casual first lady is a work in progress. Once I offered to bake cookies at home and bring them in for everyone to share, and I got looks of pure horror.

However, there are responsibilities associated with being first lady, and I take them seriously. We all have obligations. I might not want to sit down and write a speech, but if I'm going to do it, it's going to be something I can at least enjoy saying. I'm going to find something in the journey or the outcome of this role that brings me happiness. I've met some first ladies who have been amazing. They have lived this life for so long and experienced so much that they're able to give me tremendous wisdom. Their most common advice: "Don't change who you are." They reminded me that people will have expectations of who and how I'm supposed to be, and I will never ever meet them. So don't try. Lady Serita Jakes, Bishop T. D. Jakes's wife, gave me the same advice. It was some of the best I've ever gotten.

I needed to hear it, because I felt pressured to start talking a certain way and doing things I don't typically do. I feel like I've hugged every member of the church. But I don't have a passage from scripture to give you for your circumstances. I've never been that person. I love the Lord, but I'm just not the person who's going to go up to the altar with you and pray for you, because that's not something I know how to do. You need to go to my husband for that. I'm not going to conform to expectations I know I can't meet. I want to enjoy this experience, so I try to smile, laugh, and bring a sense of fun to being first lady.

I'm also not going to be subservient. I met a first lady who was like her husband's robot, and she was completely comfortable and happy in that place. If her husband told her he didn't like her nail polish, or he didn't want her to have three colors on her fingernails, she told me she would change her nails. I have a problem with that. Because he is the husband and pastor, it's his way or no way? That's not a partnership. That's a dictatorship.

I am learning to lighten up a little and let people do *some* things for me. It's so uncomfortable for me to have people constantly holding doors for me and saying, "Let me get that for you," but Keion explained that it's not only about me. He said, "You must allow some people to be of service. That's very important to them." When he said that, I understood. The people at the church weren't fawning over me to flatter me. Serving people is their love language. He said, "You can't rob them of what they need from you. They need you to allow them to serve. You must receive it and not feel like you're abusing them. This is something that they find in their heart to do for you."

That really opened my eyes. Some people truly need to serve, and they're offended if you don't let them. That completely changed how I saw the church staff. I'm still not high maintenance. I'm very honest about what I need and don't need. The staff has learned what I like and what's too much for me. But I let them do more than I used to. We seem to have found a good middle ground where everybody is happy.

One thing I have noticed about being a first lady is that some other first ladies are as uncomfortable around me as I am around them. Some are extremely conservative, so I have to be very careful what I say. Others who might not be as conservative seem outwardly like they are. If I'm going to meet a first lady for the first time, I have to read the room quickly to determine what I can and can't say. Sometimes I might go on social media ahead of time and do some research on her: *Okay, she seems a little more conservative than I thought. Let me adjust*. I'm always going to remain true to my personality, but I also have an obligation to try to represent my husband respectfully. So, if we're not in a jeans-and-blazer type of situation, I might dress a little more conservatively.

One thing I'm not interested in is spending time in the company of first ladies who are judgmental about me and opinionated about everything and everyone. I also don't enjoy spending time with people for whom everything has to revolve around the Bible. If we go to dinner, can we just talk about your favorite place to vacation and how your kids are? With some people, every conversation has to be so profound, and there are times when I'd rather not be profound and just have a nice time.

Another thing I've noticed is that many first ladies seem to be competing with one another. I'm not sure what the prize is, and I have no idea what the rules are, but there's definitely some competition going on. They downplay other first ladies and what they've got going on at their churches. They'll say, "I have way more ministries, my husband does this," and so on. It's obviously a status game, not all that different from the one I got caught up in when I was an NBA girlfriend surrounded by wives who wouldn't give me the time of day.

Once, I was in a room full of first ladies and I literally asked them about it. I said, "I've noticed that a lot of you seem to be in competition with each other. What's the prize? Because y'all are going to heaven, I'm sure. You all seem to have a husband already, so it ain't to win the man over. So what is it? Are you trying to win the people? Because I don't think that's working."

Obviously, no one had ever had the audacity to ask such a question, because no one answered. They all just stared at me. But I guess I shouldn't be surprised, because that sort of thing is everywhere. People are always trying to outdo each other. It's even a little comforting to know that first ladies aren't immune to ambition.

If I'm going to be first lady, I'd like to use my position to do some good, and I have already done a few things. I held an expo for businesswomen around the holidays in 2022. I threw a brunch for the ladies. It was going to be a Shaunie women's empowerment event, but I decided to make it a Lighthouse event instead, and it went over well. The ladies loved it. But now we're building something called the Dream Center, which will be part school, part gymnasium, and part theater, and I will absolutely be using that as a venue for women's events.

I'm changing the role of first lady to fit my personality. Keion has managed the whole thing with patience and good humor, which is what I would expect from him. We've adjusted together. For instance, when I told him I wasn't comfortable with the traditional formalities of the role, he said, "I want you to be comfortable. Being my wife does make you first lady, but I don't need you to conform to anything that other people think you should be. I want you to be yourself. As long as you're my wife, that's all that matters. People will have to understand that. Your first lady is not going to be what they are traditionally used to, and that's fine. Do what makes you comfortable."

That is the right answer.

Through this big adjustment, Keion always has my back. If he hears someone talk about me not understanding the church, he'll defend me gently by reminding people that I grew up in the church. But now we're able to laugh off the misunderstandings. Even the lady who's always reminding me how to stand and telling me how Communion works—I just thank her and we laugh about it later, because her intentions are good. What more can you ask for?

CHAPTER 13

LIFE AFTER DEATH

For any daughter, our relationship with our father is our first relationship with a man, and it can create the template for what our future relationships with men will look like. For daughters whose fathers are abusive or neglectful, that can be a terrible thing. For me, my relationship with my father set a precedent that was mostly good. For all his flaws as a husband, my dad was a terrific father. I've already shared some of the details about him from my childhood, from his chronic lateness in picking me up from school to his membership in the Nation of Islam, but through it all one fact remained consistent: He loved and cherished me as his little girl. So, when he got sick in 2020, I could sense that this was the end of an era in my life.

As with many older people, my father didn't really "get sick" suddenly. His health declined steadily over a couple of years due to heart failure and type 2 diabetes. It was frustrating watching his health worsen, because we all knew there were things he could do to prolong his life, like drastically changing his diet. Given how advanced his diabetes was at that point, I don't know if it was reversible, but changing his diet surely would have improved his health and given him more time. But he just would not cooperate. The older he got, the more stubborn he got.

As you can imagine, that drove us all a little crazy. I might tell him, "Dad, you know you can't have ice cream or pie anymore," but he would sneak off and eat those foods regardless. His defiance didn't stop in the kitchen, either. There were also medical procedures he could have had that might have prolonged his life, but he refused them. At one point, his cardiologist wanted to put a stent in one of his coronary arteries to improve blood flow and reduce the risk of a heart attack—a common procedure that's highly effective and very safe. He refused that too. He didn't believe the procedures would help him or fix anything. If he was going to die, he was going to die on his own terms.

Frustrated by his stubbornness, we—my mother, my sister Cori, my brother Tyrik, and I—found ourselves constantly fussing about the decisions he was making. His behavior didn't make any sense. If you had simple ways available to you to improve your health and longevity and to enjoy more time with your loved ones, why wouldn't you take advantage of them? But after a while, we got tired of the fussing and frustration, and we accepted that no matter what we said, Dad was going to do what he was going to do. I had a choice to make. I could have a battle of wills with my father and try to get him to make different choices, or I could accept that this was his choice and try to make the most of the time I had left with him.

I chose the latter, and I began a stage of life that we all know is coming, we all dread, and that we all do our best to endure.

Some people call death "*the* great leveler," because eventually it affects everyone. It doesn't matter if you're a celebrity, rich, or successful, eventually death comes calling. We all feel that more keenly now since the pandemic, because so many of us knew or worked with people who were struck down in the prime of life by the virus. But it's still relatively easy to keep death at arm's length until it shows up at your door. I'm forty-eight years old as I'm writing this, and that age range—late forties to midfifties—is the time when most of us must deal with the hard reality of our parents getting sick or dying. For years I knew that *intellectually*. But now I *felt* it. Just like everyone else, I was about to lose something I would never get back. I would just have to do it with as much grace and strength as possible.

If you've ever had an ill parent, you know life becomes all about who travels where and when. Over the year and a half that our father was sick, my sister, brother, and I juggled our own lives and the life of a caregiver. Along with our mother, Cori and Tyrik were still in Los Angeles, but I had moved to Houston, so seeing my dad meant hours in airports and on planes. Thankfully, my kids were all grown and independent (except for Me'arah, and she was in high school and could mostly take care of herself), so it was a little bit easier to juggle all the stuff I had to keep in the air: *Basketball Wives*, my increasingly serious relationship with Keion, my family, and my own physical and mental health. Still, it was a time of relentless stress and worry.

As Dad's body failed, he was in and out of the hospital quite often. First, when I got the call that he'd been admitted, I would drop everything and go to L.A. For example, his blood pressure might spike, which meant spending one night in the hospital at least, and I'd be on a plane. The doctors would give him medication and get his blood pressure back down, and he'd go home, and then I would go home. But that wasn't sustainable for me. It was exhausting. As Dad went into the hospital more and more, I finally said to Cori, "Please, just let me know when I need to come and when I don't need to come." Which was a polite way of saying, *Please let me know if it looks like this is the end, so I can be by our father's bedside and say goodbye.*

One reason the experience was so hard was that while I had decided I wouldn't argue with my father about his stubbornness, it still drove me crazy that he wouldn't do *anything* to extend his life. I couldn't understand it. Maybe he was thinking, "I'm dying, and I just want to live how I want to live until I can't live anymore. I want to eat what I want to eat." I don't know what he was thinking, but it is painful to watch someone allow themselves to die when you just want them to be here. Sometimes when I flew out, I would bring the kids, and it was like they were begging him to listen. But he would just say, "I hear you, but I know what I'm doing."

Privately, without meaning to, I found myself getting angry with him. I'd think, *We want you here, and you're not fighting like we want you to fight.* But then I realized I was making it about me, and I had no right to do that. I'd gotten used to being in control, and here was a situation where control was out of the question. When it came to my father, I had only one responsibility, which was to make his passing as loving and peaceful as it could be. Eventually, I accepted what was happening on its own terms: *He's a grown man, he's lived his life, he's okay with whatever's happening right now, and he's earned the right to leave this life the way he wants to.*

After that, he and I had some quiet conversations in which he told me, "I want you to be happy. Don't stop living life just to baby me. There's nothing you could do. You've done everything you could do." He was right about that. We did everything we could—everything he would *allow* us to do.

But it wasn't enough. It never is.

Another thing COVID-19 changed for most of us was that we developed a new appreciation for the hard work and sacrifices of care-givers, from nurses to unpaid family members. My experience with my father drove home just how punishing it can be to be a caregiver, even at a distance. I would talk to my mom every day, but when I saw her name come up on my phone, I would immediately wonder if she was calling to tell me something terrible had happened. But as tense and stressed out as I was, my sister's experience was much, much harder.

I had the luxury of distance, but Cori was there in L.A., and while she was working as a flight attendant, her world became taking care of our dad. She put her life on hold, consumed with trying to help our dad get better. Whatever she needed to do to keep him here with us she was going to do, and if that meant backing off her career for a while, or missing her children's games and activities, she would do it. Even now, with our father gone, that year put a strain on our re-lationship. I think she might feel like I didn't experience what she experienced because I wasn't with our father twenty-four-seven—like soldiers who went off to war and came back unable to relate to people who couldn't know or understand what they had gone through.

To this day, my relationship with my sister is different from what it was before our father died. The funny thing is, if I saw her right now, things would seem normal. She's not treating me differently. I'm not treating her differently. There's no anger. She loves me and the kids, and she's there for us. But we don't talk like we used to. We were so close, and now it feels like there's this distance between us. It feels like she's retreated from things so she can mourn, and her mourning isn't the same as my mourning. She's six years younger than I am, and her experience with our father was different from mine.

As I've said, I was Daddy's little girl. My experience with him was him taking me places around the city and bringing me gifts and treating me like a little lady. It was . . . chivalrous. Sure, he was late all the time and he hung out in sketchy places with sketchy people, but he treated me like gold. Cori came along when Dad was older, and they were not as close in the beginning but grew closer as she entered her twenties. Toward the end of his life, they grew even closer. She got a different version of our father than I did, an adult-to-adult version.

In a strange way, I was lucky. While it was terrible to watch my father go gradually and spend the last days of his life in a hospital, at least I had time to talk with him a lot before the end. We spent hours talking when I came to L.A., even though during the last couple of months of his life he would go in and out. I didn't care. I was content just to be there. Sometimes he would talk about memories from his childhood, but I was able to have the conversations with him that I wanted to have.

During his last few days, he wasn't conscious or able to respond, but I was able to sit on the edge of his bed and talk and just say what I needed to say. I told him what a great daddy and grandad he was, and how happy I was with Keion. Being able to do that brought me a great deal of peace.

On March 8, 2022, Vester Lee Nelson passed away at the age of seventy-four. I let the world know via Instagram on March 15:

> *The first man I ever loved is gone. For some reason it doesn't seem real at times. But in those moments that it gets tough, I hear your voice.*
>
> *One thing about my dad is he loved a good time. It was going to be nothing but laughs mixed with him "kickin some knowledge" lol. He left us with SO MANY beautiful memories.*
>
> *My goal is to continue making you proud. . . . I Love you Daddy.*

One thing you learn about death is that life doesn't wait for it, and life didn't wait for me to grieve before it tapped me on the shoulder and said, "Uh, you've got things to do." Not to put too fine a point on it, I had a wedding to plan, whether I wanted to or not.

While my father was dying, the resort was calling me because the last deposit to hold all our hotel rooms was due. Talk about a surreal experience. I could have handed that over to Keion and he would've taken care of things, but he was busy communicating with the hospital and mortuary on behalf of our family. I didn't want to just dump everything in his lap. Eventually, it all just became overwhelming and I had to let Keion take charge for a couple of weeks. That wasn't easy for me, but I just didn't have the mental or emotional capacity left to take care of business and mourn at the same time.

After that brief break, the demands kept coming, so I had to keep functioning and manage the endless details. Talking to my sister while we were planning our dad's funeral, I apologized because I didn't know how to disconnect Dad from the wedding planning. Everything was muddled together. When the resort started pressing me for payment, I called them and said, "My father passed away yesterday. Can I get another day?" They said, "We can give you twenty-four hours." That was as far as their sympathy extended. They cared about getting their money, and dead father or no dead father, if we didn't pay on time they would give our rooms to someone else. It was a harsh reminder that the rest of the world keeps turning even while it feels like your world has stopped.

That was one of the toughest parts of my father's passing for me, because I didn't know what to do. I was planning to marry the most wonderful man in the world, the love of my life, and I was wondering, *Do I just cancel everything that's going on that's so wonderful right now to sit in this place of grief and pain? I don't know what to do in that place.* My emotions were all over the place.

Was it acceptable for me to feel joy at my upcoming wedding? I didn't want to hurt anyone by seeming happy when everyone expected me to be in tears. That's the trouble with grief—it's different for everyone. There's no one way to grieve losing somebody; there are millions. For example, you will not see my mom cry. If she needs to cry, she won't let you see it, because she doesn't want you to see her hurting. So, during the wedding planning, my mom stayed as upbeat as possible, saying things like "Get this wedding done. You need to be happy. We got this, it's okay." She was incredibly supportive at a time when you would think a woman who'd just lost her husband of fifty-four years would be falling apart.

Meanwhile, I was sure my siblings were looking at me and thinking, *How can you keep moving like this? We're suffering and you're planning a wedding!* I was very worried that I would look insensitive, yet the whole time I was mourning in my own way. It was impossibly hard because I just didn't know what to feel, when to feel it, and who to feel it in front of.

The thing is, I'm sure that if my father could have told me what he thought about the whole affair, he would have said, "Have your wedding. I'm fine. Be happy." He loved having a good time, and all he ever wanted was for me to be happy. In the end, I suppose it doesn't matter. Keion and I had our wedding, it was fabulous, and I'm incredibly happy. That's exactly what my father would have wanted.

Naturally, losing my father has made me think a lot about losing my mother. My mom and I talk every single day now. We laugh, and I ask her if she needs anything. If she ever does, I make sure it's there. It's also important for me to be sure there's nothing I need to tell my mom, nothing I need to get off my chest. I think I've achieved that. If I got the call right now that my mom had passed away, I would grieve, but I don't think I would have any regrets.

I want her to be here as long as possible, but when it's time for her to go, I would rather have her go right away instead of to be like my dad was, sick and miserable for the last year and a half of his life. He didn't want to be helped to the bathroom or helped out the door or helped in and out of the car, even though he needed the help. He was a very prideful man. To watch his ego and his pride be damaged by all that, I wouldn't wish that on anyone. If I had to choose between someone going quickly and not being able to say goodbye but being spared the suffering, and someone lingering like my dad did but having time to say goodbye, I'd choose going quickly. Death isn't the worst thing. Suffering is.

Still, I think about losing my mom all the time. I know I'll lose her at some point, and I hope I have as long with her as I can get. I'd like to think I'm prepared, but I know when the time comes, I won't be. The one thing I can do is make sure I don't have any regrets and I've said all the things I need to say.

That's why I talk to Mary every day, even if I know she's not going to have much to talk about because we just talked the day before. That doesn't matter. What matters is that's what makes her smile and makes her happy. Even if she just needs five minutes of my time to know how much I love her, I'll find that time every day.

CHAPTER 14

LETTING GO
AND MOVING ON

It was August 2020, and I was a mess. I was overwhelmed with anxiety and worry to the point where I couldn't sleep and was in tears a lot of the time. You know this if you followed me on social media. Why? A few days earlier, I had participated in a time-honored parental ritual: dropping my children off at college. I had taken my beautiful daughter Amirah, and my precious, "When did this child become six foot ten?" son Shareef, to start attending classes and playing basketball at Louisiana State University in Baton Rouge, where their father went to school. Shareef had started his college basketball career at UCLA, but when the coach who had recruited him was fired, he made the decision to leave UCLA for LSU.

I was feeling a pain that mothers have felt since forever: I was saying goodbye to some of the children who had been my joy and preoccupation for half my life. Yes, I still had Shaqir and Me'arah at home back then, but this was a preview of what was coming: *If these two can leave, the others will leave too.* The idea left an empty place in my heart that was made even worse by the fact that my children were leaving at a time when COVID was raging. I was mourning, but I was also terrified.

When your kids go away to college, it's probably the first time they'll be living away from home for an extended period. And college isn't summer camp. They don't leave for a few weeks, come home, and resume life as before. College is the beginning of a new phase of life for them and for you. When they come home for holiday breaks or summer vacation, they've already got their eyes on next semester, graduation, a year abroad, or their first job. You, your home, your rituals, the things you used to do together . . . they aren't the center of your world anymore, no matter how badly you want them to be.

I've known parents who took their kids to school and then sobbed for weeks when they got home, and that includes some fathers. We're proud of them, but they're still our babies and they don't need us the way they used to. Even though that's the way things are supposed to be, it hurts. It's a reminder that things change, that we're losing things we can't ever get back, that we're really getting older, and that we can't protect them from some of the heavy stuff the world can lay on us. We must give them the privilege of having those experiences for themselves. The word *bittersweet* comes to mind.

I understand. My children are my entire world. I've always put them first, before the demands of *Basketball Wives*, before business and charity work, before everything. There's a reason the first word on my website bio says "Mother." That's the most important part of my identity. So, I knew that even if I was dropping off Amirah and Shareef at LSU during normal times, as soon as I drove away from those dorms with my kids waving goodbye—or, more likely, having forgotten about me in their excitement and confusion—I would be in the middle of a mascara-ruining ugly cry before I even hit the on ramp to Interstate 10.

I sobbed all the way back to my hotel.

As you've seen, my life has been a consistent process of self-reinvention and discovering strengths I didn't even know I had. Today's Shaunie is very, very different from the Shaunie I was when I met Shaquille, or the Shaunie I was when I started *Basketball Wives*. Not only that, this Shaunie is also still learning. If you had asked me four years ago, when I was still very single, if I had myself all figured out, I would have said yes. I had done a lot of self-reflection and a lot of challenging work, and I thought I had really learned who I was. Then I met Keion and got married, and I've learned that I'm still learning about myself. It's a process that you never complete, and part of that process now is learning to let go of the past and look to the future.

Today, I'm constantly learning things about myself and having aha moments. I'll find myself thinking, *Oh my God, you really do think this way.* Just like that, I have something to work on in this new life and relationship. For example, I'm extremely independent, but now I have a man in my life who's a gentleman and wants to open doors for me and be chivalrous toward me. I haven't had a man do that in a long time, and for a while I wasn't sure how to handle it. Keion is the type of man who doesn't even want me to go to the gas station. He'll say,

"Let me put gas in your car. I don't want you to go to the gas station by yourself. It's dangerous."

I've programmed myself to be completely self-reliant, and it's taken me a while to see something amazing: *I don't have to be!* I'm with a man who can care for me without threatening my independence. So, I've softened a bit. If Keion wants to take care of me, I can allow him to do that. You might laugh and say, "Poor Shaunie, that must be so hard!" but it's not so easy for me.

In this new season in my life, I've been thinking a lot about my purpose. What service can I offer women and people in general? I had never really thought about that before. Sometimes the answer changes, but for right now, I'm finding new avenues to serve others and enjoying every bit of it. I might not be able to quote scripture and change your life, but I can share my experiences, my journey, and my growth with people and hope they take away something that encourages them to be a little bit better.

I can teach by example, too. When I lost my father in 2022, one of the ladies who used to be on *Basketball Wives* texted me her condolences. She and I used to have a great relationship when she was on the show, but through the course of her leaving the show our relationship soured. I can't pinpoint what exactly happened or why, but in that moment, I messaged her back and after I thanked her, I apologized for anything I ever did to anger or hurt her. I felt better. I knew I did the right thing. Whatever she decides to do with that is up to her, but I like knowing that whether my gesture inspires her to pay it forward or not, I put a little bit more compassion and understanding into the world.

I don't sit around and worry about the feelings of every person who's ever been mad at me. But I'm in this place now where I'll think,

I used to have a relationship with this person. This person was my friend. I at least owe them an apology. Even if I feel like I didn't do anything, I want to be a better person and at least extend an olive branch. If nothing else, I'm releasing myself from guilt or resentment. For me, part of this new season of life is about becoming more of what my loved ones need me to be. In my personal life, that's my purpose.

In terms of my professional life, I have all kinds of ideas and new projects I'd like to work on. I'd like to start a business or two. And, as I said earlier, since our wedding millions of people have shown interest in Keion's and my relationship—how we've been able to combine our lives and careers with relatively little friction. To answer those questions, we did what everyone is doing today: We started our own video podcast called *The Groow Zone.* At the time I'm writing this we've filmed one sneak-peek episode that went over very well, so by the time you'll be reading this, odds are the podcast will be going full speed.

We want *The Groow Zone* to be a place where we help people listen and, of course, grow. We'll talk about a little bit of everything— relationships, marriage, faith, reality TV—but from our shared life perspective. As we always tell people, we're not experts on anything, and we're not therapists, but we've had lots of experiences and we think people can learn from them.

We hope to take the podcast on tour—to travel around and do a series of shows in front of live audiences, where we can take questions and interact with people. That would be a lot of work, but it also sounds like a lot of fun. And now that we're both published authors, we would also like to write a book together sharing our thoughts on love and relationships.

As I mentioned in the chapter on being a first lady at Lighthouse, I've also had my eye on the women's empowerment space for a while. While my previous event was held under the Lighthouse name, I'm starting my own women's empowerment program within the church. It's called HerSay, and it's a women's ministry. We'll hold different events and activities to highlight women's success stories, motivate women, and enhance women's skills and talents. I also put on a sort of business expo during the holidays in 2022 called Cocoa, Conversations, & Commerce, where we served cocoa and highlighted women-owned businesses. People shopped for Christmas gifts and learned about the women and their stories. It was extremely successful, and we had a great time.

I also threw a live event geared toward women and relationships. We had more than one hundred and fifty people in the room, and we sat and had conversations about relationships where people got up and talked about their experiences. You might have a woman and her husband who had been married for thirty years giving advice, and then a single guy wondering why he was having no luck meeting someone. We had a series of very intimate, real conversations.

I hosted a brunch where I was able to share my story and take questions. It was an intimate talk among women about everything from business to health care, mental health to finding true love. All this falls under the HerSay brand. I even plan to start a division that's a mentoring program for young girls. I want to build it into a movement at some point.

Of course, I haven't turned my back on television. After producing the wedding special, I can see Keion and me doing more TV projects together, and I'm still pitching shows of my own. There's the possibility of a reality show based on my life, my marriage to Keion, and my awkward transition to being a first lady. Stay tuned for that.

Basketball Wives keeps going strong—as I wrote earlier, we're casting an Orlando spin-off. But in keeping with my journey, I'd like to grow beyond the *Basketball Wives* formula for television. I don't know if the networks would agree with me right now, because reality TV is so profitable, but I'd like to do television that makes people feel good. I think we're all a little tired of drama, fighting, and flipping tables, especially after going through the trauma of COVID.

I'd like to take *Basketball Wives* to a more elevated place. I'm constantly talking with the people at BET and saying, "Could we do something more than have these ladies at the pool all the time? Can we just have them laugh? Most women I know are trying to help each other or lift each other up, and if there is drama, it doesn't require throwing a chair." I want to reel in the ridiculous level of violence and fighting on the show, but something else needs to change. During the 2022 season of the show ratings were horrible, and it's because the network pushed for a lot of made-up content and manufactured bitchiness. They forced these women to care about things they didn't care about, and to have conversations about things they didn't want to talk about. Viewers could smell inauthenticity and chose to tune out.

When I went back and watched the season, I asked myself, *Why are they talking about the same things over and over again? Why do they sound so immature?* Since I'm behind the scenes and talking to the ladies, I know the answer. The network kept sending back notes saying things like, "Could you have them have that conversation about sex again in another restaurant and add one more cast member to it?" This is supposed to be reality TV. The network should only be sending notes like, "That scene is too dark," or "The sound wasn't right." We're becoming scripted television, and that's not the show our fans fell in love with. It's not the show I wanted to create. These ladies are better than that. They have real stories to tell. They don't need to have their stories manufactured.

BET took over from VH1 in early 2023, and *Basketball Wives* will no longer air on VH1. That's probably the best move for the franchise since COVID, at least. BET executives have said the right things in our meetings. I'm excited to move forward with them. I think we can finally go back to telling real stories and talking about real situations in real time and giving these remarkable women the platform I originally wanted them to have.

There's one more part of this season of my life that I don't like to think about, and it goes back to when I took Shareef and Amirah to LSU. I'm going to be an empty nester soon, and I'm dreading it. My father's death has already forced me to acknowledge that time is marching on, but by the time you read this, Me'arah, my baby, will be eighteen and about to graduate high school. She'll go to college, and I want her to do that. But it's been more than *twenty-five years* of some small person roaming around my house playing, doing homework, or asking me for something. I'm not sure how I'll handle the silence.

Ready or not, that future is here. Most of my children are grown and have moved out of the house, living their own lives, and thriving.

Myles is in Los Angeles. Shareef is in Las Vegas, playing in the G League. Amirah and Shaqir are in Houston, and it doesn't seem like they're planning to go anywhere anytime soon, so I get to see them more often. Me'arah is still at home, so I still get to be mom for a while longer, but the clock is ticking. I'm in contact with my other kids nearly every day, but it's not the same. A huge phase of my life is ending, and while it's liberating in some ways, it's also a little depressing.

Me'arah is the baby, so I'm sure she wants her independence. She wants to go away to college—she doesn't know where exactly, but she doesn't want to stay home, and that's fine. But if I'm being honest, I try not to think about it, because it makes me sad. Not having a child in my house is like living in a foreign country. I'm thankful I found a partner, because if I was alone, I might be packing and going with her. I can't imagine her not turning a corner and saying, "Mom?" or me not turning a corner and saying, "Hey, you ready to go?" It already took me a lot of adjusting to get used to not having kids everywhere; instead, I've learned how to juggle staying connected with the ones who are out of the house. But she's my baby. She was never supposed to grow up, even if the other ones did. She was always supposed to stay the baby and stay with me.

When I look at them and see what amazing young adults these five have become, it makes things a little easier. I know we'll always stay connected. I want them to experience life, too. I don't want to hinder them from having learning experiences and exploring everything life has to offer. They've earned the right to do that. How many parents can have five children and have no horror stories to tell? I don't have any surprise grandkids, no one's gone to jail, and no one is addicted to anything. Every one of my kids is a successful human being, and I have a great relationship with each of them. I'm incredibly blessed.

People now ask me if I'm ready for them to have children of their own, and I always say, "Yes, but not right now!" Give it ten years, maybe. I'm gonna need the time to find a really cute name to use instead of Grandma.

So the phases of life just keep coming, whether I want them to or not, and whether I'm prepared or not. But it's hard not to feel blessed by the life I have, even if every blessing has come at a cost. But that's the way of things. What you have is only worth what you pay for it. I've built an incredible professional career, but I probably wouldn't have had the motivation to start *Basketball Wives* if I hadn't gotten divorced. I'm married to a man so marvelous that I pinch myself just thinking about the fact that he's my husband, but I might not have recognized him for who he is if I hadn't gone through so much pain and despair in my previous marriage.

I've raised five children who humble me with their intelligence, maturity, and generosity, but I don't know if I could have been half as good a mother without the hard lessons my mother and father taught me. And while I'm a leader, an entrepreneur, and a first lady of a church, the self-knowledge and growth that's made those roles possible has come from sleepless nights, dark depression, anger over self-inflicted denial and dependency, and disgust at compromises I've made along the way. In other words, I have scars, but those scars have made me who I am.

It took me many, many versions of myself to get to where I feel good about me. I definitely see where all the ups and downs, bumps and bruises have molded me into the woman I am today. I am very comfortable with that woman. I like who I've become. I'm human, so I know I'll still be upset, sad, or angry from time to time. But I've learned that how I react to challenges is my decision. Life might still catch me off guard sometimes, but my goal is to be a little better every day—to be intentional about my decisions as well as my reactions.

All in all, I like who I am *becoming*. Because the version of Shaunie who's finishing this book is just the latest version. Tomorrow, I'll be someone a little different. Because we never stop learning, growing, and discovering who we are. That's what keeps us engaged, excited, and eager to see what comes next!

ABOUT THE AUTHOR

Shaunie Henderson, a trailblazing media mogul, philanthropist, creative visionary, and culture-shifting producer, stands at the helm of Amirah, Inc.—a powerhouse production company renowned for creating one of reality television's most successful and genre-defining franchises, acknowledged by *Time* magazine as one of the "50 Most Influential Reality TV Seasons of All Time." Hailing from Los Angeles, Shaunie is not only a seasoned entrepreneur but also a devoted mother, shaping the lives of her five children—Myles, Shareef, Amirah, Shaqir, and Me'Arah—with whom she shares a foundation of love, sharing, and encouragement, recognizing these as crucial elements for nurturing emotionally healthy and happy children in today's complex society.

Beyond her professional and maternal roles, Shaunie proudly supports her husband, Pastor Keion D. Henderson, founder and Senior

Pastor of The Lighthouse Church in Houston, Texas. Together, they exemplify a harmonious blend of entrepreneurship, family, and spiritual leadership. Shaunie emerges not only as a force in the media industry but also as a beacon of inspiration for those who seek to balance success, family, and community values.